OFFICIAL SQA PAST PAPERS WITH ANSWERS

HIGHER

BUSINESS MANAGEMENT
2008-2012

SQA

First exam published in 2008.
Published by Bright Red Publishing Ltd, 6 Stafford Street, Edinburgh EH3 7AU
tel: 0131 220 5804 fax: 0131 220 6710 info@brightredpublishing.co.uk www.brightredpublishing.co.uk

ISBN 978-1-84948-283-7

A CIP Catalogue record for this book is available from the British Library.

Bright Red Publishing is grateful to the copyright holders, as credited on the final page of the Question Section, for permission to use their material. Every effort has been made to trace the copyright holders and to obtain their permission for the use of copyright material. Bright Red Publishing will be happy to receive information allowing us to rectify any error or omission in future editions.

HIGHER

2008

[BLANK PAGE]

X234/301

NATIONAL QUALIFICATIONS 2008	WEDNESDAY, 14 MAY 9.00 AM – 11.30 AM	BUSINESS MANAGEMENT HIGHER

Candidates should attempt **all** questions in Section **One** and **two** questions from Section **Two**.

Read all the questions carefully.

100 marks are allocated to this paper.

50 marks for Section **One** and

50 marks for Section **Two**.

Answers are to be written in the answer book provided.

SECTION ONE

This section should take you approximately 1 hour 15 minutes.

Read through the following information, then answer the questions which follow.

SWEET TASTE OF SUCCESS SPOILED BY SUPERMARKETS

Background

Lees' main business is the manufacture of confectionery and bakery products. It can trace its roots back to 1931, when confectioner John Justice Lees allegedly botched the formula for making a chocolate fondant bar and threw coconut over it in disgust, producing the first macaroon bar. Its customers include major food retailers, food service and catering companies and other food manufacturers. It operates from 2 modern manufacturing sites in Coatbridge and Cambuslang. Lees now employs 155 staff at its Coatbridge plant, along with around 60 at the Waverley Bakery in Cambuslang, which Lees acquired for £600,000 at the beginning of 2003. Macaroon bars and snowballs have been adored by Scots for 75 years—but Lees was going nowhere until former Bell's whisky boss Raymond Miquel became Managing Director and saved the company from bankruptcy.

In recent times supermarkets have put the squeeze on Lees, but the snowball maker still plans to enter more overseas markets and expand through takeover bids. Increases in labour, transport and raw material costs cannot be passed on to consumers because of cut-throat price discounting among the major supermarket chains. Raymond Miquel said "The multiple retailers just won't accept price rises and haven't done for several years, which means we have to keep looking to new markets and new products."

The company experienced some bad times in the 1980s when sales dropped to an all time low. In 1993, the company had a balance sheet worth £350,000 and almost folded with debts of over £5 million owed to suppliers, the Clydesdale Bank and the Inland Revenue. The economic situation at the time didn't help with a worldwide recession. However, they have turned themselves around and built a new factory. Now the products are not only doing well in Scotland but are being sold in the USA, the Netherlands and Ireland. Even the King of Tonga can't get enough of them! This has resulted in a number of supermarkets and confectioners running out of stock of Lees Macaroon Bars as the company has had problems coping with increased demand.

Modernisation and transformation

Miquel saved Lees from liquidation in 1993 when he acquired the company from Northumbrian Fine Food for around £1 million. In 1993, Lees had a number of unprofitable product lines which were eventually shed by Miquel. In the 12 intervening years, however, the company has transformed itself—announcing in 2005 a rise in annual profits of 5 per cent and sales up by 9 per cent. In comparison, in 2002, the company saw sales rise but profits fall.

Miquel, by his own admission, inherited 2 run-down factories producing a handful of old-fashioned products and a very nervous workforce who were concerned for the future of their jobs. Miquel felt that many of the operations aspects of the business were in a

mess. His first decision was to tackle the firm's unprofitability. Many senior managers were not performing to the standards that Miquel expected and as a result were dismissed from their posts. Next to be targeted by Miquel was the outdated 1930s style packaging. Despite working hard, the sales staff were not making enough of a profit margin for the company. This was addressed by recruiting new sales staff and training existing staff.

Miquel describes his style of management as "a bit more hard nosed" than most managing directors and this has caused conflict with some of the long term managers at Lees.

The present situation

Since Miquel took control, sales of macaroon bars have surged, and Lees now sells 2·5 million every year. This represents more than 40 per cent of the company's total confectionery sales. No less popular are Lees snowballs, now selling more than 50 million a year in the UK.

Today Lees is sitting on a massive £6 million in reserve, has no debt and a large overdraft facility. It plans to expand the business overseas and to target other businesses for takeover. Miquel forecasts all kinds of possibilities to diversify, such as restaurants, upmarket tearooms and retail outlets. However, Miquel believes this will be a relatively slow process. Lees will only acquire companies which will add to their profitability, giving them further opportunities to expand in the food industry.

Lees has now floated on the stock market, just over a decade after it stared liquidation in the face. It can only be a matter of time before Miquel's Lees story amazes further!

Adapted from *http://thescotsman.com/business/*

Marks

QUESTIONS

You should note that although the following questions are based on the stimulus material, it does not contain all the information needed to provide suitable answers to all the questions. You will need to make use of knowledge you have acquired whilst studying the course.

Answer ALL the questions.

1. Identify the problems faced by Lees. You should use the following headings. (Please identify problems only, solutions will not be credited.)
   - Marketing
   - Human Resource Management
   - Finance
   - Operations   **10**

2. Organisations often use an entrepreneurial structure. Explain the advantages and disadvantages of an entrepreneurial structure.   **4**

3. Lees could use the Internet to market their brand name to overseas customers.
   Describe the benefits of using the Internet to market products.   **5**

4. Lees' Board of Directors has identified growth as a strategic objective.
   (a) Explain internal factors which could be taken into account prior to an organisation setting strategic objectives.   **4**
   (b) Describe **3** tactical decisions that could lead to growth.   **3**

5. Lees' management use ratios to analyse financial data.
   (a) Describe ratios which could be used to ensure appropriate levels of profitability and liquidity are maintained.   **5**
   (b) Describe the limitations of using ratio analysis.   **3**

6. Lees changed the packaging of their products which made them more eye-catching and appealing to consumers.
   Explain **5** other methods of extending a product's life cycle.   **5**

7. Wholesalers buy goods in large quantities directly from manufacturers.
   Discuss the advantages and disadvantages to a manufacturer of using a wholesaler.   **5**

8. Discuss the role of appraisal and its ability to motivate staff.   **6**

                                                                                         (50)

[END OF SECTION ONE]

SECTION TWO

Marks

This section should take you approximately 1 hour 15 minutes.

Answer TWO questions.

1. (a) Describe how both horizontal and vertical integration could allow an organisation to become even larger and more profitable.   **5**

    (b) Describe methods a limited company could use to finance a successful takeover.   **4**

    (c) Explain why firms use loss leaders as a pricing tactic.   **3**

    (d) Describe the methods available to a Public Relations department to improve the image of an organisation.   **5**

    (e) Many organisations group their activities by function.

    Discuss other methods an organisation could use to group their activities.   **8**

    (25)

2. (a) Employees may undertake industrial action in an attempt to force employers to meet their demands.

    Describe types of industrial action that employees could take.   **4**

    (b) Explain possible effects that prolonged industrial action could have on an organisation.   **5**

    (c) (i) Distinguish between delayering and downsizing.   **3**

    (ii) Explain the benefits to an organisation of using outsourcing.   **4**

    (d) ICT is used to help head office communicate effectively with branches in remote areas of the country.

    Explain how modern technology can be used to communicate effectively within an organisation.   **6**

    (e) Describe **3** types of production.   **3**

    (25)

3. (a) Describe how stakeholders could make use of financial information provided by an organisation.   **7**

    (b) Describe **4** causes of cash flow problems.   **4**

    (c) (i) Identify and explain **3** economic factors that can affect the profitability of a business.   **6**

    (ii) Describe **4** other external influences that can affect the success or failure of a business.   **4**

    (d) Discuss the advantages and disadvantages to organisations such as Asda of selling own brand products.   **4**

    (25)

[Turn over

Marks

SECTION TWO (continued)

4. (*a*) Organisations spend vast sums of money developing new products.

    Describe the stages that take place before a new product is launched onto the market.   **6**

    (*b*) Explain the advantages to an organisation of using market segmentation.   **4**

    (*c*) Explain the purpose of the Advertising Standards Authority.   **2**

    (*d*) (i) High quality and reliable information is essential if a manager is to make effective decisions.

        Describe the characteristics of high quality, reliable information.   **4**

        (ii) The Data Protection Act 1998 is the legislation which covers information stored on computers about individuals. Describe the main features of the Data Protection Act.   **5**

    (*e*) Explain the role of testing in the selection of new staff.   **4**

    (25)

5. (*a*) (i) Describe how the introduction of Quality Management (formerly TQM) techniques could ensure a quality product or service.   **5**

        (ii) Explain how the Human Resource Department can help to ensure that a quality product or service is produced.   **4**

    (*b*) (i) Describe the JIT stock control system.   **2**

        (ii) Describe the advantages and disadvantages of using such a system.   **5**

    (*c*) Describe how a manager could evaluate the effectiveness of a decision.   **4**

    (*d*) Describe the advantages and disadvantages of a wide span of control.   **5**

    (25)

[END OF QUESTION PAPER]

2009

[BLANK PAGE]

X234/301

NATIONAL
QUALIFICATIONS
2009

MONDAY, 18 MAY
9.00 AM – 11.30 AM

BUSINESS
MANAGEMENT
HIGHER

Candidates should attempt **all** questions in Section **One** and **two** questions from Section **Two**.

Read all the questions carefully.

100 marks are allocated to this paper.

50 marks for Section **One** and

50 marks for Section **Two**.

Answers are to be written in the answer book provided.

SECTION ONE

This section should take you approximately 1 hour 15 minutes.

Read through the following information, then answer the questions which follow.

700 Staff Made Redundant At Fopp

Background

Fopp was set up in the early 1980s by Gordon Montgomery. It grew from a market stall in Glasgow into the largest independent music chain in the country with a flagship store on London's Tottenham Court Road. Over the past 7 years it has expanded from 5 to 105 stores, specialising in offbeat music, sold at "no-nonsense" prices of £8–£12. Fopp became the third largest high street music retailer employing over 1,000 staff.

With rising interest rates putting pressure on the company, the recent closure could not be halted. Gordon Montgomery said they had not anticipated the continual increase in interest rates when purchasing Music Zone, a rival retailer.

The Fall of Fopp

Approximately 700 workers at Fopp were made redundant by the company's administrators Ernst & Young. They said that the redundancies were "unfortunate" but that Fopp was not in a position to resume trading.

Fopp's stores were shut after the administrators were called into the struggling business. The 105-branch retailer was forced to close after being plagued by price reductions, coupled with stiff competition from online retailers and supermarkets. Jobs were cut nationwide, with London's Tottenham Court Road store the worst hit – losing 30 members of staff. However, store managers across the country are to keep their jobs while Ernst & Young assess the prospects for re-opening. Also attributed to Fopp's problems was the purchase of 67 Music Zone stores, placing added pressure on the firm's cash flow.

"We urged anyone with a genuine interest in taking on stores as going concerns to contact us immediately," said Tom Burton of Ernst & Young. "However, confidence in the music industry is at an all time low and we could not attract financial backing from any entrepreneurs."

The Music Industry

The music industry as a whole had felt the competitive and economic pressures in a very cut throat market. Despite rapidly increasing demand, music producers and sellers have struggled to maintain sales revenue, as downloads and illegal copies drive down volumes and sales margins. Yet music has never been played so widely, with loudspeakers sprouting in every public space, and earphones adorning every ear not glued to a mobile phone. However, global CD sales have fallen 10% to £1·7bn, according to the International Federation of the Phonographic Industry (IFPI).

Fopp fell victim to the same pressures that forced Tower Records to file for bankruptcy. Fopp saw a near-halving of pre-tax profits (to £48·1m) in 2006–7, as it fought a book and record discount war with e-tailers and big supermarket chains.

Fopp kept their stock of CDs for sale on the shop floor and, unlike supermarkets, CDs were kept in their actual case. This left it open to theft by customers and staff in the stores found it very difficult to control. Originally Fopp purchased their CDs from Poland cheaper than they could find suppliers in the UK. When Poland joined the EU the wholesale price of CDs rose to a similar cost of that in the UK and Fopp lost their source of cheap CDs.

CD trade was hit by the growing popularity of music downloads which doubled to more than 10% of the market in 2007 according to the IFPI. Continued growth in high-quality illegal copying, despite attempts to curb it by countries that have joined the World Trade Organisation, also hit the industry hard. While digital music sales are estimated to be growing at 50% per year, sales of CDs are tailing off, with the UK and US leading the fall. In fact UK music sales actually fell 8% in 2006 to £1·2 bn.

The next generation of technology is set to prompt further growth in demand for downloads. The music industry's inability to protect its legal rights remains a massive threat to profitability. Although some fans are responding to artists' appeals to keep paying for what they're playing, tougher encryption may be needed before there is any boom in sales.

Final Fopp

Fopp was offered a last-ditch rescue package in a move that could have ensured the company's survival saving hundreds of jobs. HBOS, Fopp's bank, offered to install a Chief Restructuring Officer at the retailer to implement a turnaround strategy. The move, which would still have led to a number of store closures, is understood to have been declined by Fopp's management. The bank is also understood to have offered to extend Fopp's overdraft if the retailer accepted its proposal.

A source close to Fopp said the offer of restructuring came when accountants from Ernst & Young had already been reviewing the company's performance. "It was too late," said the source.

Like music itself all good things come to an end. Fopp it seems has gone past its sell by date. From its original and much loved idea amongst music lovers, the Glasgow company failed to gain support from stakeholders and closed its doors.

Adapted from www.scotsman.com
www.bbc.co.uk

[Turn over

Marks

QUESTIONS

You should note that although the following questions are based on the stimulus material, it does not contain all the information needed to provide suitable answers to all the questions. You will need to make use of knowledge you have acquired whilst studying the course.

Answer ALL the questions.

1. Identify the problems faced by Fopp and the music industry. You should use the following headings. (Please identify problems only, solutions will not be credited.)
   - Marketing
   - Finance
   - Operations　　　　　　　　　　　　　　　　　　　　　　　　　　**10**

2. (a) Initially Gordon Montgomery was a sole trader, however, he eventually operated Fopp as a private limited company. Explain **3** reasons why an organisation would become a private limited company.　　　　**3**

   (b) Describe how **5** different stakeholders of Fopp could influence the organisation.　　　　**5**

3. The management of Fopp use financial budgets. Explain why managers use cash budgets.　　　　**5**

4. Describe **3** pricing tactics that could be used when an organisation attempts to break into a new market.　　　　**6**

5. The use of the most up-to-date technology is extremely important in the music industry.

   Describe the benefits to an organisation of investing in new technology.　　　　**5**

6. Fopp employed a large number of temporary and part-time staff.

   Discuss the effects on an organisation of employing staff on temporary contracts.　　　　**4**

7. (a) A decision was made by Fopp's directors to purchase the Music Zone stores. Describe how a manager could assess the effectiveness of a decision.　　　　**4**

   (b) Explain the factors that could affect the quality of a decision made by a manager.　　　　**4**

8. Discuss the importance of quality inputs in the operations process of an organisation.　　　　**4**

　　　　　　　　　　　　　　　　　　　　　　　　　　　　　(50)

[END OF SECTION ONE]

SECTION TWO
Marks

This section should take you approximately 1 hour 15 minutes.

Answer TWO questions.

1. (*a*) It is becoming more popular to purchase products online. Explain the advantages to an organisation of selling products over the Internet. — 4

   (*b*) Distinguish between the terms quantitative and qualitative information. — 2

   (*c*) The introduction of new technology may cause unrest in the workplace. Describe **4** forms of industrial action. — 4

   (*d*) Describe **4** methods of field research. — 8

   (*e*) (i) Draw a diagram to illustrate how you would manage stock control effectively (your diagram should be correctly labelled). — 3

   (ii) Describe different stages involved in setting an appropriate stock level. — 4

   (25)

2. (*a*) Most organisations group their activities by function. Describe the advantages and disadvantages of functional grouping. — 5

   (*b*) Discuss the effects of outsourcing on an organisation. — 5

   (*c*) Explain how external factors may affect an organisation. — 6

   (*d*) (i) Describe the recruitment process that may be used by a Human Resource Department. — 5

   (ii) Discuss methods that an organisation could use to ensure their staff stay motivated. — 4

   (25)

3. (*a*) Describe the problems that can occur when using only accounting information to analyse performance. — 4

   (*b*) Describe the actions an organisation could take to improve the following ratios:

   • Net Profit Percentage

   • Current Ratio — 6

   (*c*) Discuss the effects on an organisation of branding their products. — 6

   (*d*) Some organisations still sell their original product a number of years after it was first launched.

   Explain how extension strategies can prolong the life of a product. — 6

   (*e*) Justify why strategic decisions are made by senior managers. — 3

   (25)

[Turn over

Marks

SECTION TWO (continued)

4. (*a*) Discuss the effects of widening the span of control. **7**

    (*b*) (i) Describe the different forms of training that an organisation could use. **6**

         (ii) Describe the costs of staff training. **4**

    (*c*) (i) Describe **3** types of production available to organisations. **3**

         (ii) Explain the factors that would affect the choice of production method used. **5**

         (25)

5. (*a*) Explain how the following legislation could impact on an organisation:

- Freedom of Information Act 2002
- National Minimum Wage Regulation 1999
- Employment Rights Act 1996. **6**

    (*b*) (i) Describe **3** different methods of growth. **3**

         (ii) Describe and justify **3** sources of finance that could be used to expand a business. **6**

    (*c*) Describe the advantages and disadvantages of gaining approval from the British Standards Institution (BSI). **4**

    (*d*) Many organisations segment their market by gender eg male or female.

Describe **6** other methods that an organisation could use to segment their market. **6**

         (25)

[END OF QUESTION PAPER]

[BLANK PAGE]

X234/301

NATIONAL QUALIFICATIONS 2010

MONDAY, 17 MAY 9.00 AM – 11.30 AM

BUSINESS MANAGEMENT HIGHER

Candidates should attempt **all** questions in Section **One** and **two** questions from Section **Two**.

Read all the questions carefully.

100 marks are allocated to this paper.

50 marks for Section **One** and

50 marks for Section **Two**.

Answers are to be written in the answer book provided.

SECTION ONE

This section should take you approximately 1 hour 15 minutes.

Due to copyright restrictions the Case Study and Question 1 have been removed.

Marks

QUESTIONS

Answer ALL the questions.

1. This question has been removed due to copyright restrictions.

2. (*a*) Describe the role of the Human Resource department in employee relations.   5

   (*b*) Explain the effects that poor employee relations could have on an organisation.   4

3. Discuss the advantages and disadvantages of customer grouping.   4

4. Describe the factors that would result in a quality decision being made.   4

5. Describe and justify **4** methods of direct selling that could be used by an organisation.   (A different justification must be used to support each description.)   8

6. Explain the reasons why some organisations produce a mission statement.   3

7. (*a*) Compare the objectives of a private sector organisation with those of a public sector organisation.   4

   (*b*) Describe the different interests **5** stakeholders may have in an organisation.   5

8. Describe the main features of a matrix structure.   3

(40)

[END OF SECTION ONE]

Marks

SECTION TWO

This section should take you approximately 1 hour 15 minutes.

Answer TWO questions.

1. (*a*) Describe **5** factors an organisation might take into account before choosing a supplier of raw materials.   5

    (*b*) Discuss the advantages and disadvantages of empowering staff within an organisation.   6

    (*c*) Describe the main characteristics of high quality information.   5

    (*d*) Explain the role of the Finance department in an organisation.   4

    (*e*) Describe the factors an organisation would take into account before choosing a channel of distribution.   5

    (25)

2. (*a*) Discuss the effects of ICT on an organisation.   5

    (*b*) Discuss the advantages and disadvantages of using a structured decision making model.   7

    (*c*) Appraisal has identified poor performance for a member of staff.

    Describe the actions that a manager could take to improve the employee's performance.   4

    (*d*) Describe a selection process that an organisation could use to ensure it employs the best workers.   4

    (*e*) Many companies are now classed as multinationals.

    Explain the advantages and disadvantages of operating as a multinational.   5

    (25)

3. (*a*) Describe the reasons why organisations focus on research and development.   4

    (*b*) Describe the benefits to an organisation of staff training.   5

    (*c*) Explain how various methods of extending a product's life cycle can increase sales.   6

    (*d*) Describe the advantages and disadvantages of methods of physical distribution that a producer could use to get their product to consumers.   5

    (*e*) Discuss the effects of becoming part of a franchise.   5

    (25)

[Turn over

Marks

SECTION TWO (continued)

4. (a) Describe **4** different sources of long term finance available to a private limited company.   **4**

    (b) (i) Describe accounting ratios managers could use.   **6**

          (ii) Explain the limitations of using accounting ratios.   **5**

    (c) Describe **4** different sales promotions that could be carried out by a retailer.   **4**

    (d) Describe the uses of ICT in decision making.   **6**

                                      (25)

5. (a) (i) A manager decides to grant a worker's request to have a week's holiday.

            Identify and justify this type of decision.   **2**

          (ii) Describe **2** other types of decisions and give an example of each.   **4**

    (b) (i) Describe different methods organisations can use to develop a corporate culture.   **4**

          (ii) Explain the advantages to an organisation of having a strong corporate culture.   **4**

    (c) Distinguish between job production and flow production.   **5**

    (d) Organisations use various forms of advertising media to bring their products to the attention of consumers.

        Describe and justify different forms of advertising media.   **6**

                                      (25)

[END OF SECTION TWO]

[END OF QUESTION PAPER]

[BLANK PAGE]

HIGHER
2011

[BLANK PAGE]

X234/301

NATIONAL QUALIFICATIONS 2011	WEDNESDAY, 25 MAY 1.00 PM – 3.30 PM	BUSINESS MANAGEMENT HIGHER

Candidates should attempt **all** questions in Section **One** and **two** questions from Section **Two**.

Read all the questions carefully.

100 marks are allocated to this paper.

50 marks for Section **One** and

50 marks for Section **Two**.

Answers are to be written in the answer book provided.

SECTION ONE

This section should take you approximately 1 hour 15 minutes.

Read through the following information, then answer the questions which follow.

THE DEMISE OF SETANTA

The Irish pay-TV company Setanta was placed into administration after rescue talks, designed to secure new funding, collapsed. Setanta officially ceased to broadcast in the UK in June 2009 and all of its UK staff were made redundant.

Since its inception Setanta and its financial backers had invested hundreds of millions of pounds buying UK and international sporting rights. With the hard work and dedication of its staff, a pay-TV broadcaster was created which entertained people in 3 million homes with top-class sport. Now the initial investors have lost their capital and have been left wondering what went wrong.

The first indications of financial difficulties came to light at the end of the season 2008/09, when Setanta failed to meet a scheduled £3m broadcasting rights payment to the Scottish Premier League (SPL). This resulted in the SPL cancelling its agreement with Setanta. The SPL was one of a number of sporting organisations to count the cost of the loss of Setanta's broadcasting revenue.

As a result of government legislation Setanta was forced to suspend the collection of subscription payments from customers in the UK with immediate effect. It would have been illegal for Setanta to continue to collect existing direct debits or take on new customers knowing that administration loomed.

Some of the existing Setanta investors had stated they were prepared to commit significant funds to the business if it could improve its operating performance. This meant existing contracts having to be re-negotiated. The re-negotiations made some improvements but they were insufficient to convince the investors to part with their funds.

Setanta's founders had been left focusing on trying to rescue the Irish and North American operations, which were believed to be making a modest profit. The company continued to trade under Setanta Ireland and Setanta International. Neither Setanta Ireland nor Setanta International had been heavily marketed in the UK over the previous 5 years. Setanta concentrated on its UK base during this spell resulting in a low customer awareness of the Irish and International brands.

COMPETITION – SKY SPORTS AND ESPN

Setanta operated in a highly competitive market, with Sky and the Disney owned broadcaster ESPN, both huge rivals. These rivals were prepared to bid billions of pounds to secure the rights to specific sporting events, including Sky's broadcasting of the Premiership football in England. Setanta struggled to match the bidding of its rival broadcasting giants. Both Sky and ESPN also have vastly superior marketing structures which secure huge numbers of subscribers each year.

A lack of subscription income meant that Setanta was unable to make the payments to the governing bodies of the sports to which it held the broadcasting rights. Furthermore, the recession resulted in many viewers cancelling their subscriptions and cutting back on luxuries like satellite TV. With only 1·2 million subscribers in the UK, Setanta was well short of the 1·9 million subscribers it needed to break even.

In an attempt to attract new subscribers, Setanta massively overbid to secure certain broadcasting rights. This included a £390 million bid for a 3 year deal for 46 English Premiership football games per year. The games secured by Setanta were less significant than the glamour games bought by Sky and therefore much more difficult to market to subscribers. Losing out on these glamour games had a double impact on Setanta's revenue as advertisers pulled out from agreed marketing and advertising deals.

sky SPORTS

Setanta seemed to compromise on what games were shown. They showed replays of top league games ahead of live lower league games, leaving subscribers unhappy. Setanta's camera work and technology also left many armchair fans disappointed. Setanta had fewer cameras and crews at games meaning less angles shown during matches. The use of poorer technology compared to their rival often resulted in interrupted broadcasts. Setanta's studio commentators seemed to be less comfortable in front of the camera than the Sky Sports presenters. One customer commented "I am shocked and disgusted with Setanta's (so called) 'sports' coverage". At a time when customer satisfaction should have been paramount, Setanta was failing to captivate the armchair fans.

The big winner in Setanta's demise was Sky Sports, who now have the sole broadcasting rights of the much sought after English Premiership football plus the SPL. With a virtual monopoly on football, companies are more than willing to pay Sky to show their advertisements.

Marks

QUESTIONS

You should note that although the following questions are based on the stimulus material, it does not contain all the information needed to provide suitable answers to all the questions. You will need to make use of knowledge you have acquired whilst studying the course.

Answer ALL the questions.

1. Identify the problems faced by Setanta. You should use the following headings. (Please identify problems only, solutions will not be credited.)
   - Marketing
   - Finance
   - Operations
   - External Factors   **10**

2. Describe methods an organisation could use to encourage positive employee relations.   **6**

3. Describe financial information that stakeholders could use to assess an organisation's financial position.   **5**

4. Describe and justify **3** market research techniques that an organisation could use to assess customer satisfaction. (A different justification should be used each time.)   **6**

5. Explain the effects of delayering on an organisation.   **4**

6. (*a*) Distinguish between a wide area network and a local area network.   **2**

   (*b*) Describe and justify the use of **4** types of information. (A different justification should be used each time.)   **8**

7. Discuss the use of quality standards for an organisation.   **6**

8. Describe the benefits to an organisation of using interviews prior to appointing a new employee.   **3**

                                                                 (50)

[END OF SECTION ONE]

Marks

SECTION TWO

This section should take you approximately 1 hour 15 minutes.

Answer TWO questions.

1. (a) Distinguish between a strategic decision and a tactical decision.   3

    (b) Explain the advantages of staff training for an organisation.   4

    (c) Describe the role of a manager in staff appraisal.   5

    (d) Discuss the use of just in time production.   6

    (e) (i) Explain the effects that **3** political factors could have on an organisation. (A different effect should be explained each time.)   3

    (ii) Describe **4** external factors (other than political) that could have an impact on an organisation.   4

    (25)

2. (a) Describe and justify **3** sources of finance available to a partnership. (A different justification should be used each time.)   6

    (b) Explain the reasons managers use accounting ratios.   4

    (c) Describe the main features of the Data Protection Act 1998.   5

    (d) (i) Explain the effects that branding its products could have on an organisation.   5

    (ii) Describe the stages that a product might go through prior to being launched onto the market.   5

    (25)

3. (a) Describe methods of growth.   6

    (b) (i) Explain the impact that recent trends in retailing have had on organisations.   4

    (ii) Describe the reasons why some manufacturers sell their products to retailers rather than directly to customers.   4

    (c) Explain advantages and disadvantages of becoming a public limited company.   5

    (d) (i) Describe the main characteristics of an entrepreneurial structure.   3

    (ii) Distinguish between a centralised structure and a decentralised structure.   3

    (25)

Marks

SECTION TWO (continued)

4. (*a*) Compare the use of functional grouping with product grouping. **5**

   (*b*) Explain internal problems that can exist when managers try to make effective decisions. **5**

   (*c*) Describe different payment systems available to an organisation. **5**

   (*d*) (i) Describe and justify **3** forms of testing (other than interviews) used in the selection process. (A different justification should be used each time.) **6**

   (ii) Discuss the use of internal sources of recruitment. **4**

   (25)

5. (*a*) Explain the benefits of using Information Communications Technology for a multinational organisation. **5**

   (*b*) Describe factors an organisation should consider when trying to encourage a positive corporate culture. **5**

   (*c*) Explain the advantages to an organisation of using a structured decision making model. **5**

   (*d*) Describe reasons why an organisation would use cash budgets. **5**

   (*e*) Explain the advantages and disadvantages of using job production. **5**

   (25)

[END OF SECTION TWO]

[END OF QUESTION PAPER]

[BLANK PAGE]

[BLANK PAGE]

X234/12/01

NATIONAL QUALIFICATIONS 2012	WEDNESDAY, 30 MAY 1.00 PM – 3.30 PM	BUSINESS MANAGEMENT HIGHER

Candidates should attempt **all** questions in Section **One** and **two** questions from Section **Two**.

Read all the questions carefully.

100 marks are allocated to this paper.

50 marks for Section **One** and

50 marks for Section **Two**.

Answers are to be written in the answer book provided.

SECTION ONE

This section should take you approximately 1 hour 15 minutes.

Read through the following information, then answer the questions which follow.

Peter Scott & Co. Find a Buyer

Peter Scott & Co., the Hawick based textile manufacturer, was sold as a going concern to UK clothing company Gloverall in May 2010. Almost 120 of the Peter Scott & Co. staff were made redundant when it fell victim to the economic downturn. The remaining 20 staff were transferred to the Northampton based Gloverall, who made their name manufacturing duffle coats.

Samuel Lee, Gloverall director, said, "Gloverall is delighted to acquire a business with such a rich heritage and brand presence. We are currently reviewing our intentions to recommence full production of Peter Scott & Co. products in Hawick."

Peter Scott & Co.

Peter Scott founded the company in 1878 but success came slowly. However, Peter Scott's energy and perseverance, plus his practical knowledge and business ability, meant the business expanded. Peter Scott & Co. was still manufacturing in Hawick over 100 years later. During that time it went on to become one of Scotland's best known exporters.

Right from the beginning Peter Scott always strove to buy the best in wool, silk, cashmere and cotton. This drove the cost of production up, meaning a high price needed to be charged in order to make a profit. This policy of purchasing expensive high quality materials continued until the company went into administration in 2010.

Unusually, for a modern manufacturing organisation of its size, it was still a private limited company. This prevented the company from raising much needed finance through the sale of shares on the stock market. Any investment had to come from the private sale of shares, limiting the number of potential investors.

The company, even from its humble beginnings, had always maintained close links with sporting and cultural activities in the UK. Peter Scott & Co. supplied a great deal of their clothing to the golfing world and in May 2010, Colin Montgomerie, the Ryder Cup Golf Captain, teamed up with the company to promote an exclusive range of golfing knitwear. This type of expensive promotion was required to keep the exclusive brand image. However, this was to be the last of the expensive promotional activities and extravagant spending carried out by the company.

Present Situation

Despite having an excellent reputation and strong brand, Peter Scott & Co. suffered heavily from increased overseas competition. Lower wages paid by overseas firms, meant they could charge lower prices for similar products. The worldwide economic slowdown in 2010, plus the reduction in spending on luxury items in the UK,

contributed to Peter Scott & Co. being placed under administration.

This resulted in 120 redundancies taking place and the company directors working closely with local and national government agencies to save the remaining jobs. The Scottish Government attempted to help the company directors by setting up discussions with several parties who had an interest in purchasing the company. However, these discussions were not successful and failed to save the vast majority of jobs.

In an attempt to save the company, local Conservative MSP, Mr John Lamont, contacted the Scottish Government Finance Secretary. However, the UK National Budget, announced by the Government in July 2010, saw savage cuts in all areas of Government spending. This meant that there were no Government funds available to save struggling companies.

Gloverall's Plans for Peter Scott & Co.

Gloverall revealed in August 2010 that it wanted to employ 60 people within two months. The firm's Finance Director Walter Goulding said, "We are continuing to employ the initial 20 people from Peter Scott & Co., but are now looking to build back up the local workforce." He added, "The administrators had more or less decimated the workforce. There were no knitters or production staff left which left us in a poor situation to begin with. But the Peter Scott brand is an excellent product and we want to get production up and running again in Hawick as soon as possible".

Before Gloverall resumed manufacturing in Hawick they had to look closely at the production facility. The building was old and unsuitable for modern manufacturing practices. Also, the existing machinery at the Hawick factory needed upgrading to incorporate the latest technology.

Mr Goulding said, "Our firm is very big in the Far East and we want to further develop these markets. The plan is to invest in the production facility at Hawick and as the business grows, hopefully we will be in a position to expand. The 'Made in Scotland' label is very important to our future success". It is hoped for the Borders textile industry and Hawick in particular, that the success of Gloverall continues.

Sources: The Scotsman, May 2010

Drapersonline.com

Gloverall.com

[Turn over

QUESTIONS

Marks

You should note that although the following questions are based on the stimulus material, it does not contain all the information needed to provide suitable answers to all the questions. You will need to make use of knowledge you have acquired whilst studying the course.

Answer ALL the questions.

1. Identify the problems faced by Peter Scott & Co. You should use the following headings. (Please identify problems only, solutions will not be credited.)
    * Marketing
    * Finance
    * Operations
    * External Factors　　　　　　　　　　　　　　　　　　　　　　　　**10**

2. Other than funds, describe the types of assistance a Local Enterprise Company could provide for an organisation.　　　　　　　　　　　　　**4**

3. Describe **2** pricing tactics that an organisation could use when selling an exclusive product.　　　　　　　　　　　　　　　　　　　　　　　**4**

4. Describe the **3** main types of decision that an organisation could make.　　**3**

5. Distinguish between centralised and de-centralised decision making.　　**5**

6. Explain the benefits to an organisation of introducing ICT.　　　　**5**

7. (*a*) Describe the purposes of sales and production targets.　　　　**3**

    (*b*) Describe the actions that could be taken to overcome cash flow problems.　　**5**

8. Explain the problems that can arise from "under" and "over" stocking.　　**5**

9. Discuss the effects of introducing flexible working practices.　　　　**6**

　　　　　　　　　　　　　　　　　　　　　　　　　　　　　　　　(50)

[*END OF SECTION ONE*]

SECTION TWO

Marks

This section should take you approximately 1 hour 15 minutes.

Answer TWO questions

1. (*a*) Describe the advantages and disadvantages of product endorsement.   **6**

(*b*) Discuss the use of customer grouping for an organisation.   **4**

(*c*) Describe and justify **3** sources of finance that could be used by a partnership. (A different justification must be used each time.)   **6**

(*d*) Describe the advantages of e-commerce to an organisation.   **5**

(*e*) Describe the features of high quality information.   **4**

(25)

2. (*a*) Describe different types of organisational relationships that can exist within a business.   **4**

(*b*) (i) Describe quality management systems that can be used within an organisation.   **7**

(ii) Describe **3** different types of production that could be used by an organisation.   **3**

(*c*) Describe **3** accounting ratios and justify their use. (A different justification must be used each time.)   **6**

(*d*) Explain how different methods of growth can lead to increased sales or profits.   **5**

(25)

3. (*a*) Describe the benefits of different types of information.   **4**

(*b*) Describe **5** stages of the recruitment process used by most organisations.   **5**

(*c*) Describe **3** different employment contracts and justify their use. (A different justification must be used each time.)   **6**

(*d*) Discuss the effects of outsourcing on an organisation.   **5**

(*e*) Explain the advantages and disadvantages of using a wholesaler.   **5**

(25)

[Turn over

SECTION TWO (continued) *Marks*

4. (a) Describe different forms of industrial action that an employee could take. **5**

   (b) Describe the main features of the Equality Act 2010. **3**

   (c) Describe the features of an effective stock control system. **5**

   (d) (i) Compare the use of "time rate" with "piece rate" for paying employees. **3**

   (ii) Describe other employee payment systems that could be used by an organisation. **4**

   (e) Explain the advantages and disadvantages of using a structured decision making model. **5**

   (25)

5. (a) Describe the main characteristics of a multi-national corporation. **4**

   (b) Describe the possible objectives of a private limited company. **4**

   (c) (i) Describe the final accounts that would be produced by an organisation. **3**

   (ii) Describe reasons why a competitor would make use of another organisation's final accounts. **2**

   (d) (i) Describe the **4** main stages of the product life cycle. **4**

   (ii) Describe the effect of each stage on profits. **4**

   (e) Distinguish between:
   - quota sampling and random sampling **2**
   - product led and market led organisations. **2**

   (25)

[END OF SECTION TWO]

[END OF QUESTION PAPER]

[BLANK PAGE]

Acknowledgements

Permission has been sought from all relevant copyright holders and Bright Red Publishing is grateful for the use of the following:

An article adapted from 'Sweet taste of turnaround success' by Alistair McArthur from The Scotsman, 22 May 2006 © The Scotsman Publications Ltd. (2008 pages 2 & 3);

The logos for Lees of Scotland and The Waverley Bakery and photographs from Lees Confectionery. Published by Lees Food Plc. (2008 pages 2 & 3);

An article adapted from 'Deal in the bag as Fopp snaps up Music Zone stores' by Hamish Rutheford, 6 February 2007; 'Stores closed, staff unpaid and jobs at risk as Fopp goes into administration' by Hamish Rutherford, 30 June 2007 and 'Niche record store chain must lose 700 jobs in fight for survival' by Fergus Sheppard, 4 July 2007, all taken from The Scotsman © The Scotsman Publications Ltd. (2009 pages 2 & 3);

An article adapted from 'Fopp is biggest independent chain,' 6 February 2007, and 'Music chain Fopp sheds 700 jobs,' 3 July 2007, taken from www.bbc.co.uk (2009 pages 2 & 3);

The logo for ESPN © ESPN EMEA Ltd (2011, page 3);

The logo for Sky Sports © British Sky Broadcasting Ltd (2011 page 4);

The article 'Peter Scott & Co finds a buyer', 11 July 2010, taken from http://www.scotsman.com/business/peter-scott-amp-co-finds-a-buyer-1-816940 © The Scotsman Publications Ltd. (2012 page 2);

An extract and images from Gloverall.com © Gloverall Plc. (2012 pages 2 & 3);

An extract taken from Drapersonline.com © Drapers (2012 pages 2 & 3).

SQA HIGHER BUSINESS MANAGEMENT 2008–2012

BUSINESS MANAGEMENT HIGHER 2008

SECTION ONE

1. Marketing
   - Producing only a handful of old-fashioned products.
   - Had outdated 1930s style packaging.
   - Competitive market.
   - Low profit margin eg cut-throat price discounting.

   Human Resource Management
   - Anxious and nervous workforce concerned for the future of their jobs/demotivated workforce.
   - Many senior managers were not performing to the standards that Miguel demanded.
   - Miguel's style of management is a 'bit more hard nosed' causing conflict with some of the long term managers.
   - Inadequate sales staff.

   Finance
   - In the 1980s sales dropped to an all time low.
   - In 1993 they nearly folded with high debts/liquidation/bankruptcy.
   - The company had a balance sheet worth just £350,000.
   - The world wide economic recession.
   - Sales staff were also not making enough of a profit margin for the company
   - Pre tax profits fell.

   Operations
   - Lee's couldn't cope with increased demand.
   - Inherited 2 run down factories.
   - Miguel felt that many of the production and operations aspects of the business were in a mess.
   - Increase in costs *(max of one cost)*.

2. Advantages
   - Decisions are made by experienced managers of the organisation.
   - Decisions are made quickly as managers do not consult staff.
   - Staff know who they are accountable to.

   Disadvantages
   - Is difficult to use in larger businesses.
   - Top managers carry a heavy workload/burden.
   - Does not allow for initiative from staff.
   - Demotivated staff as they are not included in decision making.

3.
   - Can sell its products on the Internet, ecommerce **or** customer benefit of on-line shopping eg free delivery, online discounts etc.
   - Increased potential market to become worldwide.
   - Consumers can order 24/7.
   - Customers can leave their details on company website.
   - Customers can gain information about the products.
   - Market research can be carried out/on-line questionnaires.
   - Can research information on competitors or suppliers.
   - Gives the image of an up-to-date company.
   - Hyperlinks with other sites.
   - Quality of internal information.

4. (a)
   - Size of the organisation, smaller firms' strategic objectives will be of a smaller nature than multi-national companies.
   - Company Policy, eg social and ethical responsibility.
   - Shareholders' points of view.
   - Whether a private or public sector organisation.
   - Internal financial situation.
   - Technological factors.

   (b) *Any three from:*
   - Open new branches.
   - Offer internet shopping.
   - Target new market segments.
   - Launch a new range of products.
   - Vertical integration.
   - Horizontal integration.

5. (a)
   - Gross Profit % – measures the gross profit, on each sale, from buying and selling.
   - Net profit % – measures the profit after expenses, on each sale.
   - Mark Up – measures how much has been added to the cost of the goods as profit.
   - Return on capital employed – measures the return on investment in the business.
   - Current ratio – shows how able a business is to pay its short term debts.
   - Acid test ratio – ability to pay short term debts after stock is deducted.

   (b)
   - Information is historical.
   - Does not take into account external factors eg recession.
   - Does not show the staff morale.
   - Does not take into account recent investments.
   - Does not take into account new products launched.
   - Can only compare like organisations with like, eg size, market etc.

6. *Any five from:*
   - Improve the product – eg lighter, new features etc.
   - Alter price – eg increase/decrease price.
   - Change the method of advertising – eg from TV to radio.
   - Change the use of the product – eg Lucozade once was used to reenergise ill people, now used as a sports drink.
   - Introduce line extensions to the product – eg different flavours, sizes, formats etc.
   - Change the name of the product – eg Opal Fruits to Starburst, Marathon to Snickers.
   - Alter the place the product is sold – eg selling on-line.

7. Advantages
   - Saves on a number of smaller deliveries.
   - Administration costs are reduced.
   - Less money tied up in stock.
   - Less stock goes obsolete.
   - Wholesalers may label the product.
   - Wholesalers break product down into smaller more saleable size.
   - Wholesalers can give market research direct to manufacturer.

   Disadvantages
   - Loss of control of how the product is presented.
   - Less profits as wholesaler makes profit, ie using middle men.
   - Costs involved in producing point of sale merchandising for wholesalers.

8. • Appraisal should give feedback on the review of an employee's past performance.
   • It should involve a discussion about expectations and targets.
   • Is an opportunity to support development needs of employees.
   • Can be used to assess employees' potential for promotion.
   • It may involve bonus schemes or be linked to pay.

   Motivates staff by
   • Improving communication channels between managers and staff.
   • Should increase job satisfaction as employees will have a better understanding of how to do their job.
   • May improve loyalty to the organisation if positive rewards are given.
   • Allows for a feeling of personal satisfaction if targets are met.
   • Training and development in itself can be motivational as staff feel valued.
   • Could be demotivational if negative aspects focused on.

SECTION TWO

1. (a) <u>Horizontal integration</u>
   • Can use economies of scale and reduce unit cost of products.
   • Can dominate the market as a larger single organisation.
   • May allow for higher prices to be charged as competition is reduced.
   • Reduction in costs. *(a maximum of one)*
   <u>Vertical integration</u>
   • Profits are increased by cutting out the 'middle men'.
   • Stock can be cheaper due to backward integration.
   • Guaranteed source of supplies and prices of stock.
   • Reduction in costs. *(a maximum of one)*

   (b) • Share Issue – shares issued on the stock market.
   • Bank Loan – a loan paid back over time/with interest.
   • Commercial Mortgage – a loan secured against property owned by the organisation.
   • Sell Assets/Land – sell unwanted assets to raise funds.
   • Venture Capitalists – obtain a loan from a venture capitalist who will receive a share in the organisation in return.
   • Retained Profits – use retained profits from previous years to fund the takeover.
   • Debentures – loans paid back over a period of time with interest.

   (c) • Brings customers into the shop to buy the products.
   • Customers then buy other products which are normally priced.
   • Profits are made on the whole amount a customer purchases.
   • Creates customer loyalty as customers don't go to competitors' shops.
   • Can be used in a marketing campaign.

   (d) • Use of press release to counteract bad publicity.
   • Give donations to charities.
   • Sponsor events locally and nationally.
   • Product endorsements/celebrity endorsements.
   • Publicity literature given out.
   • Give out company merchandise.
   • Use press conference – invite media to attend – 2-way interaction.

   (e) <u>Product/service grouping</u>
   • Each division will be grouped according to a product or product range.

   • Allows for an organisation to be more responsive to changes in that market.
   • Expertise is developed within each specialised division.
   • Allows management to identify poor performing products.
   • There can be duplication of resources and personnel across groups.
   • Divisions may find themselves competing against each other.

   <u>Geographical</u>
   • Grouping of resources is carried out across a geographical area, ie, Midlands, Scottish, South-East Division, etc.
   • Allows to cater closer for the needs of different areas.
   • Can become familiar with local customs and cultures.
   • Is expensive with regards to administration and staffing costs.

   <u>Technological</u>
   • Organisations group their activities according to technological process.
   • Suitable for large organisations with different production processes.
   • Again duplication of resources occurs.

   <u>Customer</u>
   • Resources are organised around groups of customers with similar needs.
   • Allows for services to be tailored to each group of customers or a specific customer.
   • Builds up customer loyalty due to the personal service they receive.
   • There can be large staffing costs with this type of grouping.
   • Also duplication of resources in administration, finance, etc.

2. (a) • Strike – employees refuse to do their work and do not enter the workplace.
   • Sit in – employees are in their place of work but do not do any work
   • Work to rule – employees only undertake the exact jobs written in their job description.
   • Go slow – employees deliberately work at a much slower rate.
   • Overtime ban – employees do not do any overtime.
   • Picketing – employees protest at entrance to the place of work.

   (b) • Loss in production will lead to possible shortages in stock.
   • Loss in sales revenue may lead to liquidation.
   • Long term loss of customers who now shop at competitors.
   • Image of organisation is tarnished.
   • Damage to long term reputation of organisation.
   • Share price can fall.
   • May result in redundancies.
   • Improves working practices.
   • Facilitates change.

   (c) (i) • Delayering involves removing a whole level of management to flatten an organisation's structure.
   • Downsizing involves closing specific areas of the organisation to cut costs.
   • Purpose
   • Span of control
   • Communication
   • Efficiency
   • Cost
   • Competitiveness
   • Empowerment

(ii) • Specialist firms can carry out the work better than the organisation itself.
- The organisation that the work is outsourced to will have specialist equipment.
- Reduces costs of the area that is being outsourced.
- Allows an organisation to concentrate on its core activities.
- Organisation only pays for the activity when it is required.

(d) • Use of shared resources on LAN's – work can be done by more than one employee at different branches on the same software or file.
- Staff can have their own area or could have departmental areas where information is stored.
- E-mail – messages can be sent to more than one employee at a time.
- Attachments can be sent between employees.
- Video-conferencing – branch managers can hold meetings without leaving their office, saves costs of travel and accommodation.
- Mobile phones – used by sales person to stay in touch with head office or branches.
- Fax machines – information can be faxed from one branch to another.
- Internet – used to check company website information.
- Powerpoint used for delivering training.
- Spreadsheets – used to show charts/graphs and allow for easier analysis of information.
- Word processing – can be used to send letters, memos, notices to employees.
- Database – can be used to sort large quantities of information for use by staff.

(e) • *Batch production* – groups of similar products are made at the same time and no item in the batch goes to the next stage until the whole batch is ready.
- *Flow production* – items move continuously from one operation to the next and each part of the process leads to the completion of the final product.
- *Job production* – a one-off single product is made to a customer's specification.

3. (a) • Use ratios to check on the organisation's performance and to compare to other organisations and previous years. Use sales figures to set targets.
- Use the annual reports to decide whether to purchase shares. Use share prices to decide to buy or sell shares.
- Look at liquidity ratios to decide if they should allow credit or if they will receive payments for the goods they have sold the organisation.
- Interest in the profit figure to decide what taxation is due.
- The overall profit of the business could be used to decide on wage rises.
- Interest in the liquidity position of an organisation to ensure job safety.
- Profitability and liquidity position will be used to decide if they should be granted loans.
- Look at the level of creditors the organisation already has to make decisions on loans
- Analyse the profitability and liquidity of the organisation to make decisions on the local economy.

(b) *Any four from:*
- Too much money tied up in stock.
- Customers being given too long a credit period or too high a credit limit.
- Owners taking out too much money through drawings.
- Having high borrowings with increased rates of interest.

- Suppliers not allowing credit or very short credit period.
- Sales revenue not high enough.
- Sudden increase in expenses (one cost only).
- Capital expenditure.

(c) (i) *Any three from:*
- Inflation – increased prices or cost.
- Exchange rates – value of one currency compared to another.
- Interest rates – cost of taking out a loan.
- Recession – a slow down in the economy/fall in demand.
- Boom period – an upturn in the economy/increase in demand.
- Unemployment – fewer people working.

(ii) *Any four from:*
- Political factors – laws from both UK and EU affect organisations in a variety of ways.
- Social factors – society is continually changing and organisations must adapt to changing demographic trends as well as cultural trends.
- Technological factors – technology is continually advancing and organisations must keep up-to-date with new developments in technology.
- Environmental factors – weather changes in recent years have caused problems, also in recent years environmental issues have become increasingly important.
- Competition – the way competitors act will impact on how an organisation needs to alter the way it operates.

(d) • Own labels require very little advertising.
- Can attract customers to the store ie George at ASDA.
- The retailer does not need to produce the own brand products.
- A range of products with own labels can be sold.
- Some 'own brands' can be seen as value for money and a quality product.
- Own labels are cheaper to customers.
- Whole brands can be tarnished over one product's failure or problem.
- Run the risk of imitator brands.

4. (a) • Generate the idea through market research.
- Analyse the idea.
- Find the appropriate finance for the new product.
- Decide if product is legal/technically possible/can be produced.
- Produce a prototype.
- Test market.
- Make any required alterations.
- Full scale production.
- Advertise the product prior to launch.

(b) • Products are developed that suit a particular market segment.
- Allows price differentiation for different market segments.
- The place products are sold at will be appropriate for the particular segment.
- Advertising can be specific for certain segments.
- Promotional offers can be targeted to specific segments.

(c) • Monitors advertising in newspapers, magazines, billboards to ensure they are up to standard.
- Can have adverts changed or withdrawn if found to be untruthful or offensive.
- To investigate complaints.

(d) (i) • Timely – information is available when required and is up-to-date.
- Accurate – information does not contain errors.
- Appropriate – information is suitable to the task required.
- Objective – information is free from bias.
- Available – information is there when needed.
- Complete – information contains all the required parts.
- Concise – information is brief and to the point.
- Cost effective – information is not more expensive than it needs to be.
- Sufficient – there is enough information to make a decision.

(ii) • Information must be obtained lawfully.
- Must be accurate and up-to-date.
- Must only be held for the purpose stated.
- Must be securely stored.
- Should only be held for the time it is required.
- Needs to be altered if inaccurate.
- For a small fee individuals must be shown the information stored on them.
- Cannot be disclosed.
- Must be adequate and relevant.

(e) • Tests are used to provide further information than is obtained during an interview.
- Helps management decide a candidate's suitability for a position.
- Used to allow candidates to demonstrate skills they require for the position.
- Helps assess the natural abilities of staff.
- Can help assess personality traits in an attempt to see if a candidate will fit into the culture of the organisation.

5. (a) (i) • Constant improvement philosophy.
- Zero errors are tolerated therefore cuts down on wastage.
- All staff are committed to producing a perfect product.
- Quality circles are set up to make the processes more efficient.
- Clearly defined policies regarding quality exist.
- Teamwork is carried out at all levels.
- Staff training is an ongoing process.
- The organisation focuses on customer satisfaction.
- All processes are evaluated on a regular basis to ensure quality.
- Motivated staff should ensure a quality product/service.

(ii) • Recruitment and selection process ensure only high quality and appropriately qualified staff are hired. (*maximum of one*)
- Staff training should be carried out continuously.
- Appraisal systems are set up and carried out.
- Clearly defined roles for all staff are laid out in handbooks.
- Health and safety procedures are adhered to.
- Staff are motivated through staff welfare.

(b) (i) • JIT is a system that involves only ordering stock when it is needed and when an order has been placed.
- Stocks arrive just in time to be used in the production process.
- Goods are not produced unless an order is placed from a customer.
- Relies on efficient suppliers.

(ii) Advantages
- Money is not tied up in stock.

- Less space is required to store stock.
- A close relationship is built up with suppliers.
- Less wastage due to deterioration.
- Less wastage due to fashion changes.
- Reduces costs.

Disadvantages
- If suppliers don't deliver production is affected.
- High dependence on suppliers.
- High admin costs due to continual ordering.
- Higher transport costs.
- May lose discounts due to bulk buying.

(c) • Have the objectives been reached (ie problem solving)?
- Is the organisation operating effectively?
- Is there an increase in sales/profits?
- Has staff turnover/absenteeism decreased?
- Has staff morale improved?
- They may issue questionnaires/interview staff/ observe.

(d) Advantages
- Staff are empowered to make their own decisions and to carry out their own tasks without interference by managers.
- Less managers are required and wages are saved.
- Less levels of communication for decisions to pass through.
- High quality staff should exist.

Disadvantages
- Managers may make snap decisions as they are looking after too many employees.
- Managers' time will be at a premium.
- Managers will have less time for planning.
- Subordinates may make decisions they are not trained to make.

BUSINESS MANAGEMENT HIGHER 2009

SECTION 1

1. **Marketing**
   - Plagued by price deflation
   - Stiff competition from e-tailers and supermarkets
   - Global and UK sales of physical CDs fell
   - Economic pressures in the market
   - Downloads and illegal copies drove down margins (also finance)
   - Past its sell by date

   Finance
   - Continual rise in interest rates put pressure on Fopp
   - No financial backing from entrepreneurs due to lack of confidence in music industry
   - Struggled to maintain revenue
   - Pre-tax profits fell
   - Purchase of Music Zone put added pressure on the firms cash flow
   - Declined the offer from HBOS to extend the overdraft

   Operations
   - The music industry could not protect its legal rights
   - Refused to accept a restructuring officer
   - Loss of stock through theft by customers
   - Source of cheap CDs dried up (also marketing)

2. (a) *Any three from:*
   - Has limited liability to shareholders/owners which would reduce the risk of personal loss to the shareholders
   - Becomes larger organisation and should attract finance easier
   - Allows for economies of scale
   - Less risk of liquidation
   - Control is still not lost to complete outsiders
   - Experience and skills can be gained from shareholders

   (b) *Any five from:*
   - Manager – makes decisions on future plans of the organisation
   - Worker – can produce a quality product or service by working hard
   - Shareholder/Owners – purchase more shares
   - Customer – buy the product or service
   - Local Community – petition the organisation to make a change to environmental policies
   - Government – alter legislation
   - Banks – approves a loan
   - Suppliers – alter the price of supplies

3.
   - Managers can compare actual budgets with planned budgets and if there are any deviations make corrective action where required
   - Highlights periods where a negative cash flow is expected
   - Allows for appropriate finance to be arranged for that period
   - Allows for investment to be made in times of excess cash flow
   - Corrective action can be planned in advance of cash deficits
   - Allows managers to control expenditure
   - Used to set targets for workers and managers
   - Can be motivational for employees

4. *Any three from:*
   - High Price – price is set higher than competitors to give the image of quality and exclusiveness.
   - Low Price – price is set lower than competitors to attract customers to their product/service.
   - Skimming – price is set high initially when no competition exists, when competitors enter the market price is lowered to market price.
   - Market/Competitive Pricing – price is set at the same level as competitors, normally used for products that are identical.
   - Penetration Pricing – price is set slightly lower than competitors to attract customers, once a customer base has been created price is slowly increased to same as competitors.
   - Promotional Pricing – a low price is set for a short period of time to boost sales in the short term, possibly even making a loss on the product.
   - Destroyer Pricing – price is set very low compared to competitors and once there is no competition in the market the price is then put back up to the previous level or higher, used mainly by larger organisations to destroy competition, must have large reserves to sustain this over any length of time.
   - Cost plus pricing – where a mark up is added to the cost price.

5. Benefits
   - Increases the speed of information handling
   - Can make use of integrated systems such as fax, photocopier, e-mail, scanner all in one PC
   - Improves production methods through use of robotics and CAD/CAM
   - Improves efficiency in administrative functions
   - Enhances reputation with potential customers
   - Reduces staffing costs
   - Allows for teleworking
   - Allows for improved communications on a global scale
   - Can mean e-commerce is possible

6. Effects
   - Allows for greater staffing flexibility
   - Means there is no long term commitment from staff
   - Eases the burden on HRM department as recruitment agencies can be used
   - Reduces costs of items such as pensions and insurance payments
   - Reduces the need for long term staff training
   - Staff with the necessary qualifications can be found from an agency at short notice
   - More induction training will be required
   - Loss of continuity with customer services
   - Increases staff turnover

7. (a)
   - Evaluate the decision with their staff to gain their views on the change and if it has been successful
   - Issue questionnaires to customers to evaluate their response
   - Check to see if sales have increased?
   - Check to see if profits have risen?
   - Check to see if the situation has improved
   - Check to see if absenteeism has reduced amongst staff
   - Check to see if staff morale has improved

   (b)
   - The ability and skill of the manager – if the manager has not had proper training or not skilled enough to make decisions then a poor decision may be made
   - The appropriate use of decision making models
   - The quality of the information used to make the decision
   - The level of risk taken
   - The managers own interests
   - The finance available to implement the decision
   - The time available to make the decision

8.
   - Using high quality raw materials will lead to a quality product or service
   - Highly skilled staff will result in good customer services
   - Using up-to-date machinery will help standardise product quality
   - Should result in less products being faulty or not of a proper standard

- Should result in less customer complaints
- Should result in repeat sales
- Should result in the organisation having a good reputation
- May mean higher purchasing costs for raw materials
- Can result in high staff training costs

SECTION 2

1. (a) <u>Advantages</u>
   - The full range of an organisation's products can be shown on a website therefore the products are available for consumers to look at
   - Customers can purchase online from their own home – increase sales
   - Allows worldwide sales – global economy
   - Sales can be made 24/7
   - Reduces costs due to not requiring expensive premises or large amounts of staff
   - Customers can leave comments on websites
   - Can make use of customer details for market research purposes
   - Customer satisfaction

   (b) • Quantitative information can be measured and is expressed in numerical format. Qualitative information is descriptive and expressed in words.
   - Quantitative: easier to analyse, is factual, can be used to make forecasts or comparisons. Qualitative: can be used to find out customer opinions, can be used to make judgements on a product.

   (c) *Any four from:*
   - Strike: employees refuse to carry out their work
   - Overtime ban: employees refuse to work any overtime
   - Go slow: employees work at a slower rate than normal
   - Sit in: employees do no work while remaining at their workplace
   - Work to rule: employees only undertake the tasks which is in their job description and do nothing else
   - Picket: employees demonstrate outside the place of work
   - Lock-out
   - Boycott
   - Sabotage

   (d) *Any four from:*
   - Personal interview: face-to-face interview that can be held in the street or at a person's home.
   - Focus group: selected individuals are involved in discussions about an organisation's product or service.
   - Telephone survey: individuals are telephoned at their home and asked specific questions.
   - Postal survey: questionnaires are sent through the post to selected individuals.
   - Consumer audit: continuous market research is carried out with a selected group of consumers who record their purchases in a diary which is then analysed.
   - Hall test: individuals are invited to try out a product and then give their opinion on it.
   - Observation: customers actions and purchasing patterns are observed by trained staff.
   - EPOS: used to gain an insight into what products are selling in each store.
   - Test Marketing: product is launched on a small area to gauge the consumers' response.

(e) (i)

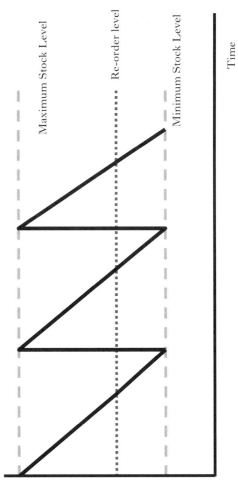

   (ii) Stages
   - Maximum stock level: The level of stock that should be held to minimise costs and involves examining storage space available and finance required for this level.
   - Minimum stock level: level that stock should not fall below as shortages could result and production could be halted.
   - Re-order level: the level which stock should be re-ordered at, takes into account usage and lead times.
   - Re-order quantity: the amount that is ordered to take the stock back up to maximum level once it is delivered.
   - Lead time: the time taken between ordering new stock and it arriving at the organisation.

2. (a) **Advantages**
   - Allows for specialisation in each functional area
   - There is a clear structure to the organisation
   - Clear lines of authority exist
   - Staff can seek support from colleagues if required
   - No duplication of resources

   Disadvantages
   - Organisational aims can be lost due to departments pursuing their own aims
   - Can be unresponsive to change in the market
   - Can produce large and unwieldy organisations

   (b) • Specialists can be used to do the work
   - Reduces staff costs in the area that has been outsourced
   - Outsourced companies will have specialist equipment

- The service can be provided cheaper
- The service can be more expensive
- The service needs only to be paid for when required
- Organisations can concentrate on core activities
- Organisations can lose control over outsourced work
- Sensitive information may need to be passed to the organisation
- Communication needs to be very clear or mistakes can arise

(c)
- Political – legislation and regulations will affect an organisation in that they need to comply with the laws of the country they operate in.
- Economic – factors such as inflation, recession/boom periods, interest rates will affect organisations in a number of ways.
- Social – changes in trends and fashions mean that organisations must continually carry out market research to see what products will sell or new products are desired.
- Technological – as technology changes organisations must keep up-to-date and this will involve a large financial cost.
- Environmental – organisations now need to attempt to be socially responsible and environmentally friendly both to comply with legislation and satisfy consumer groups.
- Competitive – organisations must continually monitor their competitors' prices and alter theirs accordingly.

(d) (i)
- Identify a job vacancy
- Carry out a job analysis
- Prepare a job description
- Draw up a person specification
- Advertise the vacancy
- Send out application forms to candidates

(ii)
- Use of staff training to motivate staff
- Give bonuses or financial rewards
- Make use of profit sharing schemes
- Organise team building days or social events
- Have staff involvement in works councils/quality circles
- Have regular consultation with staff
- Job enlargement or enrichment schemes
- Financial implications can be high

3. (a)
- Items such as new products are not shown in the accounts
- Information is immediately historical and therefore out of date
- Comparisons are limited to firms of similar size and similar industry
- External pestec factors are not taken into account
- Staff morale, turnover or skills are not taken into account
- Financial information can be slightly altered to suit an organisation's needs
- It is difficult to compare against other firms' finances as only limited accounts need be published
- Different methods of valuing stock, depreciation etc

(b) **Net Profit Percentage**
- Increase selling price
- Find cheaper suppliers
- Negotiate discounts with suppliers
- Try to reduce theft
- Also reduce wages/staff redundancies
- Reduce any particular expense
- Improve their gross profit percentage

Current Ratio
- Decrease current liabilities (pay off creditors)
- Increase current assets such as cash or bank
- If Current Ratio is too high reduce bank balance to invest in a long term investment

(c)
- Products in the brand range are instantly recognisable
- Brand loyalty can be built up
- Repeat purchases increase sales
- Is perceived to be of high quality
- Premium prices can be charged
- Can be used as a marketing tool for advertising purposes
- Makes it easier to launch new products onto the market
- Brands names can be expensive to build up
- Bad publicity can affect the whole brand
- Imitator and fake products are common

(d)
- Increased advertising of the product will increase awareness, or persuasive advertising techniques, might mean consumers may purchase more of the product or service
- Reduce the price to increase sales therefore people will buy more frequently/in larger volume
- Change the market for the product
- Re-launch the product
- Alter the product's packaging
- Change the product's name
- Find a new use for the product
- Develop a range of the same product in different sizes or shapes
- Use promotional techniques to stimulate demand

(e)
- They are long term and only senior managers would make decisions
- They have far reaching or lengthy consequences
- They shape the objectives/direction of the organisation
- They have a high financial risk
- Require a knowledge of the whole organisation and its policies

4. (a)
- Will mean more empowerment is possible – can give for both employee and management
- Allows for delegation to staff as they should be reasonably skilled
- Managers time to deal with staff problems will be at a premium
- Can place managers under stress
- Can mean workers rarely have time to meet with their line manager to discuss ideas
- Subordinates may resent having to make all the decisions
- Managers will have less time for planning
- Can result in poor decisions – both employee and organisation
- Managers are in charge of more staff
- Can be motivational to managers as can be seen as greater power

(b) (i) <u>Induction Training</u>:
- training that takes place at the start of employment
- covers items such as health and safety procedures
- background information on the organisation and job to be undertaken
- meeting colleagues
- makes a worker feel more comfortable when starting their job

<u>On The Job</u>:
- where training takes place at the place of work **or** while doing the job
- can be by demonstration or coaching
- job rotation can be used to train staff in the workplace

<u>Off The Job</u>:
- training takes place away from the normal workplace **or** at a training centre, college etc
- allows the trainee to experience the training without interference from work or colleagues
- can be more costly than on the job.

(ii) • The actual financial cost of the training
  • Production can decrease while staff are being trained
  • Posts may need to be covered while staff are away on training courses
  • Some training can be a waste of time and not beneficial to the employee
  • With more skills employees can demand a pay rise
  • Employees may leave as soon as they are trained and work elsewhere

(c) (i) *Any three from:*
  • Batch – a group of similar products are made at the same time
  • Flow – each product moves continuously along a production line from one process to the next
  • Job – an individual product is made to a customer's specification
  • Lean production (JIT)
  • Capital intensive
  • Labour intensive

(ii) • The skills of the workforce – where low skilled labour is employed, a mechanised process may prove more effective
  • The finance that the organisation has available
  • The technology available to be used in the production method
  • The size of the business
  • The actual product being made
  • The number of the product required for the market
  • Standard of quality required

5. (a) **Freedom of Information Act 2002**
  • Gives individuals the right of access to information held by public authorities therefore organisations must be prepared to accept requests for information
  • Means organisations covered by the act must be careful what information they now hold
  • Must provide the information within the specified timescale

National Minimum Wage Regulation 1999
  • States the minimum wage that organisations must now pay workers at different ages
  • Employees can take action if they are not paid the appropriate minimum wage
  • Has become more complicated to calculate wages
  • May mean younger members of staff are employed to reduce wages

Employment Rights Act 1996
  • An employee must be given a written contract of employment within 2 months of starting
  • Itemised pay slips must be given to employees
  • Maternity leave must be given to workers

(b) (i) *Any three from:*
  • Vertical Integration – organisations at a different stage in the same industry combine together.
  • Horizontal Integration – organisations at the same stage of production combine together.
  • Backward Vertical Integration – when a business takes over a supplier.
  • Forward Vertical Integration – when a business takes over a customer.
  • Diversification – organisations in completely different industries combine together.
  • De-integration/demerger – organisations cut back and concentrate on only their core activites.
  • Divestment – sell off assets or subsidiary companies to raise finance for growth.
  • Organic growth – organisations increase the number of products sold or number of outlets

(ii) *Any three from:*
  • Government Grant - does not need to be paid back if criteria for giving grant is carried out. Can be fairly large and does not need to be paid back.
  • Bank loan – paid back over a number of years with interest. Can be fairly easily obtained and can supply large amounts of funds for growth.
  • Share issues – shares are sold to raise finance either privately or publicly on stock market. Can raise large amounts of finance that does not need to be paid back immediately.
  • Venture Capitalist – provides finance for more risky ventures. Can raise finance for risky ventures and can be offset against a percentage of the firm's ownership.
  • Debentures – a loan where set interest is paid back over a period of time. Is normally paid back after a very long period of time, eg 25 years.
  • Sale of assets – assets can be sold to gain the necessary finance.
  • Retained Profits – organisations can use retained profits and invest them to allow the expansion to take place.

(c) • A specific standard can then be met for all the organisation's products
  • Levels of quality can be guaranteed to customers
  • The kitemark symbol can be used as a marketing tool
  • Can allow for a higher price to be charged
  • Is an expensive process to go through
  • Is time consuming to go through initially
  • Rigorous checks and paperwork must be kept

(d) *Any six from:*
  • age – different age groupings are used such as young or old, under 12, 13-19, 20-35, over 35.
  • occupation – the market is segmented into different types of occupation.
  • education – segmented according to the level of education attained.
  • socio-economic – socio-economic groupings are used to group customers in different economic classifications.
  • geographical – customers are segmented by area they live in.
  • cultural/religious background – various religions are used to segment the market.
  • family lifestyle – customers can be segmented into either married or single.

BUSINESS MANAGEMENT HIGHER 2010

SECTION 1

1. This question has been removed due to copyright restrictions.

2. (a) • Recognition of trade unions
    • (Written) procedures for dealing with staff complaints
    • (Written) terms and conditions for all staff
    • Make use of worker directors
    • Use of works councils
    • Ensure employees are aware of the goals and objectives of the organisation
    • The role of appraisal
    • Work with ACAS and take part in collective bargaining process
    • Take part in conciliation process
    • Take part in arbitration process

   (b) De-motivated workforce may result in:
    • Decreased productivity
    • Increased staff turnover
    • Increased staff absenteeism
    • Impact on the quality of output
    • Less co-operation of staff during periods of change could make it harder to introduce new policies or procedures

    Increased industrial action which would have:
    • Long-lasting effects on sales
    • Reduced productivity
    • Poor image of the organisation might mean potential customers and investors go elsewhere

3. **Advantages**
    • Service and product is tailor-made to customer needs
    • Promotions can be directed towards specific customer groups
    • Customer loyalty is built up due to personal service
    • Quick response to change

   Disadvantages
    • Is an expensive system, due to high staff costs
    • New staff are required if new customer group is formed
    • Duplication of resources
    • Competition between departments (either advantage or disadvantage depending on explanation)

4. • Managers who have the ability and experience to make good decisions from past experience
    • Managers who are properly trained to make good decisions
    • The quality of the information available on which to base the decision
    • Use of decision-making models
    • How much risk the managers/decision makers will take when making decisions
    • Motivation of staff to properly implement the decision
    • Finance
    • Technology

5. • Personal selling/telephone selling – products are sold by experienced sales personnel
    • Direct contact can be made to the retailer or consumer
    • Can be tailor-made to customer requirements
    • Demonstrations of the product or service can be shown

    • Mail order – goods sold via catalogues
    • Offers credit facilities
    • No need for High Street stores

    • Internet selling – making use of websites to sell products
    • Consumers can order online from offices or homes
    • Is available worldwide
    • Can be accessed 24/7

    • Specialist magazines – used to describe and sell specialised products or services
    • Customers who are sent or purchase the magazine are directly interested
    • Consumers can phone in orders or speak to specialists
    • TV Shopping Channels – where dedicated TV channels are used to sell products – allows products to be demonstrated

6. • Could be released to the press which would help market the business and its products
    • Issued to all employees allowing them to see the firm's aims and objectives linked to their roles as employees
    • Shows the organisation's plans for the future and therefore how the customers will be treated/affected
    • Will detail social responsibilities of the organisation which may attract customers to the organisation
    • Could be used to attract quality staff who would agree with the information contained in the mission statement
    • Improve the image of the organisation which could increase sales

7. (a) • Private sector organisations' objectives will focus on profit maximisation whereas public sector will require to operate within a specific budget
    • Private sector will focus on sales maximisation but public sector organisations will focus on provision of a specific product or service
    • Private sector organisations will be responsive to shareholders' opinions however public sector will have local or national government priorities and objectives
    • Increase market share/will have little or no concern with market share
    • To expand globally/operate on a local or national basis only
    • Both will look to provide a quality service
    • Both will look to be socially responsible
    • Both will try to be as efficient as possible

   (b) • Customers are interested in the best price for quality products
    • Employees are interested in job security
    • Managers are interested in future promotion prospects
    • Suppliers are interested in receiving payment for supplies
    • Banks are interested in the stability of the organisation
    • Local community are interested in the social responsibility of the organisation
    • Owners/shareholders are interested in the profits that the organisation makes
    • Government are interested in the firm complying with laws and paying taxes

8. • Normally set up to carry out a specific project
    • Will consist of different specialists from functional areas
    • Each team will have a project leader
    • Can be motivational to the staff concerned
    • Is a good method of solving complex problems
    • Gives staff increased experience in different situations
    • Is a relatively costly structure if many different teams are required
    • Can be difficult to co-ordinate staff from different areas
    • Each staff can have two managers, the project manager and their own functional manager which can cause confusion and conflict

SECTION 2

1. (a) • Do they supply appropriate quality raw materials
    • Will they deliver on time and meet deadlines
    • Can they supply the quantity needed
    • Is the price competitive with rivals/best/value
    • Do they offer any discounts
    • Do they offer credit payment terms

- Is delivery free
- Is the supplier a reliable business
- Is the location of the supplier close
- Time/Price/Quality (with description)

(b) **Advantages**
- Employees will be more motivated and will produce more
- Decisions are made quicker as the employees doing the work make the decisions
- Employees gain more skills
- Employees should come up with better ideas on how to solve problems
- Employees are better prepared for promotion
- Senior managers are freed up for strategic decision making

Disadvantages
- All employees may not want the responsibility of making decisions
- Can be a costly process to train staff properly
- Managers may not trust lower level employees to make correct decisions
- Can mean increased cost of wages to employ appropriate staff

(c) • Timely – information must be available when needed and be up-to-date
- Objective – should be free from bias
- Accurate – the information must be correct
- Appropriate – the information should be for the purpose required
- Available – should be easily obtained
- Complete – nothing should be missing
- Concise – should be short and to the point
- Cost effective – value gained from information must be greater than the cost of obtaining it

(d) • Control costs – the finance department will help control costs of an organisation which should help it be more profitable
- Monitor cash flow – will closely monitor cash flow and take corrective action if any problems arise to ensure proper liquidity
- Plan for the future – by analysing past and future trends the department will hopefully make decisions which will improve the organisation's efficiency
- Monitor performance – use the final accounts to analyse how the organisation has performed and help improve any areas of weakness identified
- Make decisions – the department will make use of the information it has to plan budgets and make financial decisions, this should help an organisation's performance and profitability

(e) • The product being sold – if the product is flowers it needs to be a fast method with appropriate facility to transport flowers
- The finance available within the organisation – if there is limited finance available then this will affect the choice of channels
- The image of the product – if the image is of a high quality product this will affect the channel that the organisation chooses
- The reliability of the other companies in the chain
- Legal restrictions
- Where the product is in the life cycle
- The organisation's own distribution capabilities
- Durability of the product

2. (a) • Increased productivity for the organisation as more is produced using ICT and robotic machinery
- Increased initial costs – the initial financial costs will be high to install the ICT

- Staff training may be required in order that staff fully utilise the ICT
- Resistance to the technology by staff
- Improved communications should exist both internally and externally
- More professional documentation will be produced
- The organisation will gain a competitive edge over its rivals who do not fully use ICT
- Teleworking will be possible for staff within the organisation as the ICT will exist to allow them to work from home

(b) **Advantages**
- Helps to identify the problem as managers are forced to go through a process
- By gathering all relevant information no rash decisions are made
- Ensures time is taken to analyse the information and develop alternative solutions
- A range of possible solutions are devised from the relevant facts and information that has been gathered
- By following this process ideas can be enhanced

Disadvantages
- Is a time consuming process to gather the information
- Decision-making process is slowed down and is not good if quick decisions are required
- Is difficult to choose from a range of solutions as it is not always clear which is best
- Gut instincts and creativity are stifled due to having to follow a rigid process

Time can be an advantage or disadvantage depending on description

(c) • Employees may be set appropriate targets
- Staff training would be given
- Could give positive feedback to the employee
- Meet regularly to discuss progress
- Allow the worker to have their say during appraisal and air any problems
- Ensure no skills the worker has are being overlooked or underused
- Appoint a mentor to a worker to give them support/advice

(d) • Compare application forms and CVs
- Send for references
- Interview the candidates
- Test the candidates eg psychometric, aptitude etc
- Second set of interviews for a short leet
- Use assessment centres for some candidates – must be different to just testing if testing given already

(e) **Advantages**
- An organisation may be given grants from governments to locate in that country and the grants will not require to be paid back improving their financial position
- Organisations will become larger which may result in them being safer from takeovers
- Can allow organisations to increase their sales which in turn should increase their overall profits
- Will allow organisations to take advantage of economies of scale and reduce unit costs of products
- Could allow organisations to employ cheaper staff which will result in greater profitability
- May help avoid legal restrictions in the organisation's own country which could allow them to sell/produce their products abroad
- Could allow for tax advantages which will increase profitability
- Will mean the organisation can avoid restrictions on imports into a country which will help overall sales

Disadvantages
- Legislation may be different in other countries which may require the organisation to alter its product/service
- Legislation may exist on how a product/service is marketed and may result in some marketing techniques having to be changed
- Cultural differences will mean that organisations have to be sensitive to different countries cultures
- Different languages will exist and this may mean that organisations have to employ specialist linguists to work with the organisation

3. (a)
- Ensure consumers are provided with the products they want – this is the only Market Research point available
- Improves on existing products
- Produces new products
- Keeps the organisation ahead of its competitors
- Finding a unique product can become very profitable
- Ensures products are safe

(b)
- The flexibility of staff to carry out different jobs is increased
- Staff ability to carry out jobs is improved
- Staff knowledge of systems and processes is improved
- This should increase productivity within an organisation
- May also increase profits if productivity is improved
- Training will be motivational to staff
- Makes the introduction of change easier for managers
- The overall image of the organisation is improved
- May be easier to recruit staff if training is given

(c)
- Improve the product – this will attract new consumers to purchase the product, or previous consumers to retry the product to find out what has been improved or if the product is better.
- Alter the packaging – this may appeal to a different market segment or may attract new customers to the product as the packing is eye-catching. *Eg*, Pepsi altered the colour of their cans to attract a younger generation.
- Increase/decrease the price – price changes can attract new consumers to purchase the product and existing consumers to purchase more of the product. Price rise may make the product seem more exclusive and attract new customers. Price decrease may mean existing customers purchase more of the product. *Eg*, lowering the price will mean families with lower income may purchase the product.
- Use a different or new advertising campaign/ advertising media – this will highlight the product in a different manner or could be eye-catching to a new group of consumers. *Eg*, change advertising from newspapers/billboards to TV.
- Change the use of the product – new use of the product will be popular with different market segments than the original use and attract a wider consumer base. *Eg*, Lucozade became a fitness drink from a health drink.
- Introduce line extensions to the product – various product line extensions will appeal to different segments and may increase overall sales.
- Change the name of the product – by changing the name, the product may appear different or better in the eyes of the consumer. Also allows for a whole new range of promotions/adverts to be launched which should attract attention.
- Alter the place the product is sold – selling the product in a variety of ways will mean a larger number of consumers can purchase the product, ie, selling online can attract a worldwide audience.

An example can be used as part of the explanation of the method.

(d) **Road**
- Refrigerated vehicles can be used to transport perishable items
- Is an easy way to get direct to a customer's location
- As road networks improve it is a quick method
- Is relatively cheap
- Can have problems with delays, road works and weather
- Cost of fuel rising makes the overall cost dearer

Rail
- Ideal for heavy products
- Less restrictions on how long the goods can be on the move
- Is more environmentally friendly than road
- Requires specialised freight terminals to load products
- Not suitable in rural areas with no rail network

Air
- Is perfect for long distances or more remote areas
- Is a faster method for overseas distribution
- Can be more expensive than road or rail
- Often still requires road transport
- Industrial action (eg, cabin crew) may prevent planes from flying

Sea
- Ideal when heavy or bulky goods are transported
- Is good for items that are not time bound
- Is a slower method than the others

(e)
- Using an established name/brand
- Reduces the risk of failure in the marketplace
- Franchiser will provide training
- Franchiser will advertise nationally
- Business idea is already successful
- Product innovation is shared
- Royalties are paid to the franchiser from profits
- Franchiser can demand exactly how a business operates
- Bad publicity can affect the whole franchise

4. (a)
- Bank loan – paid back over a number of years with interest – time or interest payable
- Commercial mortgage – paid back over a long period with interest – commercial or property must be mentioned together with time or interest payable
- Venture capitalists – invest in an organisation if a more risky venture is undertaken/may request a share in the organisation in return
- Invite new shareholders to invest in the organisation
- Local/national government grants which do not have to be paid back
- Sale and leaseback of any assets will gain finance
- Sell off unwanted assets to raise finance
- Debentures – issued to investors and interest payments are made yearly with the lump sum paid back at an agreed time – interest or repayment at end of term needed
- Retained profits of the organisation reinvested

(b) (i)
- Current ratio: – current assets/current liabilities shows the ability to pay short term debts. (Answer of 2:1 is the accepted ratio).
- Acid test ratio: – current assets – stock/current liabilities shows the ability to pay short term debts quickly. (Answer of 1:1 is the accepted ratio)
- Gross profit ratio: – gross profit/sales x 100 measures the percentage profit made from buying and selling stock
- Net profit ratio: – net profit/sales x 100 measures the percentage profit after expenses have been paid

- ROCE: – net profit/opening capital x 100 measures the return on capital for investors in a business, can be compared to other organisations or a safe investment such as a building society
- Mark Up: – gross profit/cost of good sold x 100 measures how much is added to the cost of goods for profit

(ii)
- Information is historical which means it could lead to bad decisions being made as it is out of date
- Does not take into account external factors therefore the business may have performed well during a recession
- Does not show staff morale which may be poor and the business has therefore performed well
- Recent investments are not shown which could result in future increase in performance/profits
- New products could just have been launched and again these may improve performance although ratios will not show this
- Can only be used to compare against similar organisations which may not be of great use in certain situations for managers
- Different accounting process used from one year to the next can alter ratios which could result in the wrong decisions being made

(c)
- Free samples to consumers to attempt to make them purchase the product if they like the sample
- Credit facilities given to customers to allow them to pay back over a period of time
- Bonus packs for customers that often have extra free amounts or a gift included
- BOGOF – buy one item and get another item free of charge
- Competitions used by companies which consumers enter to win prizes
- Demonstrations of products in supermarkets to let customers try products/services before purchasing
- Loyalty cards

(d)
- Spreadsheets in ICT can allow for projections to be made
- Comparisons or what if scenarios can be done using spreadsheets
- Can improve the speed of handling the information/ data with use of database or spreadsheets
- Should allow access to better quality information by using the Internet
- Larger amounts of information can be stored and retrieved quicker using databases allowing for easier access to information
- Presentation software can be used to show customers/staff information on which decision will be based
- Information can be shown in more easy to understand format using presentation/wp/dtp software
- WP software can allow for decisions to be communicated via letters
- E-mail can allow for instant flow of information/ attachments during the decision making process
- Videoconferencing can be used to have face-to-face discussions over a wide area when making decision

5. (a) (i)
- Operational decision
  - Is a decision made by a lower level manager
  - Has little or no risk
  - Is made on short term basis

(ii)
- Tactical decision is medium term/is made by middle level managers/has a slightly increased risk
  - Any appropriate example
- Strategic decision is long term/made by senior managers/has a greater risk
  - Any appropriate example

(b) (i)
- Implementing the ideals and beliefs of the owner
  - By use of symbols or logos that customers recognise
  - Staff uniforms consistent throughout the organisation
  - Uniformity of layout of offices/branches
  - Use of a phrase or motto that can be recognised by customers/used in marketing
  - How staff interacts with customers
  - Merchandising of products linked to the organisation

(ii)
- Improved customer satisfaction and loyalty as the consumers associate with that organisation due to brand/logos, etc
- Increased staff motivation as they can associate with the organisation
- Staff can move between branches/departments easier as they are aware of the practices and policies
- Staff will form an identity with the organisation which could result in reduced absences or lower staff turnover
- A single corporate identity is given to customers who will then associate with that organisation
- The organisation can be easily recognised anywhere in the world which will allow customers to feel comfortable with products/services wherever they are

(c)
- Job production is a one-off product whereas flow production is mass production
- Job production can allow for higher prices to be charged
- Specifications can be changed in job production easily whereas in flow, the same product is continually produced
- Job production is more motivating to workers whereas in flow, workers are doing the same task repeatedly
- Skilled workers are required in job production but not in flow
- Costs are spread over only one product in job production but can be spread over more than one product in flow which may reduce unit costs
- Labour costs are often higher in job production

(d) **Television**
- Large audiences can be targeted at the one time which allows it to cover all market segments
- Products can appear appealing which will attract more customers
- High profile can be maintained with regular advertising which will keep the product in the consumer's mind

Newspapers/Magazines
- National or local exposure can be obtained in order to suit the market segment or product
- Technical information can be given to customers which is necessary for some products or situations such as high specification cars
- Customers can refer back to the advert allowing consumers longer to make purchasing decisions
- Large national circulations allow for a large exposure of the product or service over wide geographical locations

Radio
- Cheaper than television therefore saves the organisation's costs
- Can have a captive audience as listeners tend not to change channels if an advert comes on
- Particular radio shows will allow for specific market segments to be targeted

Billboards/Posters
- Can have an excellent visual impact which will last in the consumer's mind
- Is frequently seen by the same consumer which will enhance the impact

Internet

- The use of links can allow exact markets to be targeted which should increase the effectiveness of the advert
- It is very easy to change adverts on websites which allows for them to be constantly changed quite cheaply

Direct Mail

- Specific market segments are targeted based on previous purchasing which may result in repeat sales
- Is a cheap method of advertising which saves the organisation costs

BUSINESS MANAGEMENT HIGHER 2011

SECTION 1

1. **Marketing**
   - Neither Setanta Ireland nor Setanta International were heavily marketed over the previous 5 years **or** low customer awareness of Irish and International brands.
   - Sky and ESPN have vastly superior marketing structures (competition)
   - This resulted in the SPL cancelling its agreement with Setanta.
   - Games secured by Setanta were difficult to market to subscribers.

   Finance
   - Failed to meet a scheduled £3m payment to the Scottish Premier League at the end of season 2008/09.
   - Rescue talks designed to secure new funding collapsed.
   - Setanta was forced to suspend the collection of subscription payments from customers in the UK.
   - The re-negotiations made some improvements but they were insufficient to convince the investors to part with their funds.
   - Lack of income due to not enough subscribers.
   - Setanta massively over bid to secure certain broadcasting rights.

   Operations
   - Setanta's camera work left many armchair fans unhappy.
   - Showing replays of top league games ahead of live lower league games left subscribers disappointed.
   - Fewer cameras and crews at games meant less angles shown during matches.
   - The studio commentators seemed to be less comfortable in front of the camera.
   - Interrupted broadcast due to poorer technology.

   External Factors
   - Sky has always been willing to pay whatever it takes to maintain its dominance of the Premiership.
   - Many organisations have now switched to rival broadcasting companies, such as Sky, to broadcast their TV advertisements.
   - Sky have a virtual monopoly on football.
   - The recession resulted in many viewers cancelling their subscriptions and cutting back on luxuries like satellite TV.

   A number of the problems are acceptable under one or more headings.

2. - Quality Circle is a group of workers who come together with management to discuss an issue or how to improve a situation.
   - Worker Director is when a lower level employee is given a place on the Board of Directors.
   - Worker Councils are made up of an equal number of employees and managers meeting to discuss issues.
   - Open Door Management Policies – managers will meet with employees at any appropriate time.
   - Participative Management Policies allow the employees to participate in the decision making of the organisation by managers consulting them and acting on their views.
   - Empowerment is when employees are given the power to make certain decisions without consulting the manager each time.
   - Appraisal is when staff meet with a line manager to discuss their progress and set targets for the future.
   - Negotiation (description required).
   - Consultation (description required).
   - Arbitration (description required).
   - Training (description required).

- Opportunities for promotion.
- Trade Union/Professional association recognition.
- Financial Rewards.

3. • Description of appropriate ratios.
- Trading account shows the profit and loss made from buying and selling stock over a period of time.
- Profit and loss account shows the overall profit or loss over a specified time period.
- Balance sheet which shows the financial position of a business at an exact moment in time.
- Cash flow statements are used to show the income and expenditure forecast over a period of time.
- Share prices show the current value of the organisation.

4. • Telephone surveys are used by organisations to call customers and gain their views. Instant feedback can be given.
- Postal survey where questionnaires are posted out to customers who complete them and return them to the organisations. Could send these out to all customers, or customers in selected areas, gaining their opinions.
- Personal interview where people are stopped in the street and asked questions. Can clarify any questions to aid understanding. Allows two way communication.
- Secondary information such as statistics on the number of subscribers to satellite TV. Easily accessible.
- Online survey.
- Interactive surveys.
- Focus group.
- Hall test.
- Test market.

5. • Cuts out a complete level of management within the organisation which will reduce the salaries paid out by the organisation.
- Managers have an increased span of control which may result in increased workload for the manager
  - increased stress for the manager
  - staff having to wait to meet with a manager.
- Communication should be improved and quicker to pass on which means the organisation will be more receptive to changes in the marketplace.
- Empowers the staff which can lead to increased motivation.
- Fewer promotion opportunities for staff which could lead to them leaving the organisation to gain promotion.

6. (a) • A LAN links computers on the same site whereas a WAN links computers outwith the one location.
  - A WAN uses external communication links and a LAN uses an internal server to link the computers.
  - A WAN will have more terminals linked to it than the LAN.

(b) • Written information is in the form of letters and memos – used for information that needs to be referred to at a later date.
  - Pictorial information is in the form of pictures or photographs – can enhance a document and make it stand out more.
  - Oral information is in the form of verbally passing on information in meetings or telephone calls – used to quickly or simply pass on information and make a point.
  - Graphical information is in the form of charts or graphs – can often be a good way to display numbers and figures or show trends.
  - Numerical information is in the form of numbers or statistics – can be good for showing comparisons or predictions of sales figures.
  - Quantitative information (description needed).
  - Qualitative information (description needed).

7. • Proves the product/service has met an agreed level of quality.
- Can be used as a marketing tool to gain a competitive advantage.
- Will give customers confidence when purchasing the product.
- May ensure repeat sales of the product.
- Involves a very lengthy and time consuming process.
- Agreed standards need to be maintained at all times.
- Will require thorough checks and audits by BSI staff to prove the standards have been met.
- Rigorous record keeping of purchases and production must be kept.
- Higher prices can then be charged.
- Less customer complaints/less returns.
- Limits waste.
- Increase sales/repeat sales/gain sales from competitors.

8. • Interviews are used to gather information on potential employees' abilities.
- Allows the organisation to compare candidates in a pressure situation.
- Gives the candidates a chance to respond to questions.
- Interviewers can compare notes to get a consensus on who the best candidate was.
- Interview styles can change allowing the organisation to examine potential candidates under different situations, ie, long leet and short leet interviews, group interviews, presentations.

SECTION 2

1. (a) • Strategic decision is long term whereas a tactical decision is medium term.
  - Strategic decision is made by directors/senior managers but a tactical decision is made by heads of department or middle managers.
  - Strategic decisions carry high levels of financial risk whereas tactical decisions carry less of a financial risk.
  - Strategic decisions shape the main objectives of an organisation whereas the tactical decisions help to put the strategic decisions into place.

(b) • Allows for a wider pool of skills to be available to the organisation which can mean staff can carry out a wider range of tasks
  - cover for absent colleagues.
  - Is motivational for staff and should mean they are happier at their work which will improve performance.
  - Can improve the quality of product/service provided which will result in improved customer relations.
  - Improves the image of the organisation which means they will attract a better calibre of worker
    - more people wishing to work for them.
  - Might reduce the number of accidents at work which will reduce any compensation or injuries to employees/customers.
  - It may be required to introduce change and will make the staff more acceptable to change
    - this will allow the organisation to be more flexible in the marketplace.

(c) • Plan out the timing and purpose of the appraisal interview in advance to ensure the employee is fully aware of the purpose.
  - Organise a suitable venue and time.
  - Control the meeting to allow the employee to have an input into the appraisal.
  - Command – may have to tell the employee that the meeting is taking place if they are unhappy with the appraisal and against it.
  - Co-ordinate the appraisal meetings before and after to ensure appropriate feedback is given.

- Delegate some meetings − peer to peer appraisal − or junior managers for experience.
- Motivate the staff with suggestions during the appraisal and give praise for any appropriate work they have carried out and targets met.

(d) • Capital is not tied up in stock and can be used elsewhere in the organisation.
- There is less warehouse space needed for stock.
- Less stock is stored which should result in less wastage.
- Theft will be reduced as stock is more tightly controlled.
- Changes in fashion or trends will have less of an impact.
- If stock does not arrive production can stop.
- May lose out on bulk buying discounts.
- There will be an increase in delivery costs as more frequent transportation exists.
- There is a high dependence on suppliers.
- May increase administration costs due to more ordering.
- Stock may have to go straight into production and may not be time to check it for quality.
- Production not started until order arrives − this can improve cash flow.

(e) (i) • Legislation − any appropriate law with an appropriate effect, ie, new laws on sale of alcohol have to be complied with or face a fine from the government.
- Taxation rates may change which will affect the profitability of an organisation.
- Level of NHS funding may affect the number of or the prices charged by private hospitals.
- Government initiatives in education have meant that private public partnerships have allowed companies to bid to build new schools.
- Credit any relevant government policy with an appropriate explanation of the affect on the organisation, ie, giving loans to banks to help with credit crunch in 2009.

(ii) • Economic factors such as a recession
  - interest rates
  - inflation.
- Social factors such as changes in trends and fashion
  - changes in patterns of employment.
- The introduction of new technology which is continually changing.
- Competitive factors such as the prices charged by a similar organisation.
- Environmental factors such as the weather/flooding.

2. (a) • Bring in another partner who will add their own/new capital to the organisation − no interest to be paid or repayment of funds (accept any advantage of a partnership).
- Bank loan − over a period of time paid back (in instalments) with interest − allows for the payments to be spread out.
- Bank Overdraft − a smaller amount for shorter period of time borrowed from bank − is useful when only needed for a short period of time and is relatively easy to arrange.
- Grant − might be possible to receive a government grant under certain conditions − does not have to be paid back.
- Retained profits from previous years − does not involve any re-payments or interest.
- Venture capital will provide finance when banks thinks it is too risky − often good for riskier investments or ideas.
- Hire Purchase.
- Leasing.

(b) • To compare current performance with previous years to see if there is any improvement.
- To make comparisons with similar size organisations in similar industry which allows them to analyse if the organisation is making appropriate GP% or NP%.
- To measure an organisation's profitability which allows for better control of expenses.
- To show if an organisation has the ability to pay short term debts which gives warnings to managers of the problems that could happen with higher than average debt ratios.
- To measure an organisation's efficiency which allows for action to be taken against inefficient areas to improve on them.
- Highlight trends so managers can be aware of profitable periods or problem periods, ie, seasonal demand.

(c) • An organisation can only hold information for a specific lawful purpose.
- They must register this purpose with the Data Protection Registrar.
- Individuals have a right to access the information held about them.
- Compensation may require to be paid if the information is inaccurate.
- The information must be accurate (needs description).
- The information must be up-to-date.
- There must be appropriate security measures in place to safeguard the information.
- Information should only be held for as long as necessary.

(d) (i) • Ensures products are easily identified by consumers and they will purchase their product and not a rival's.
- To launch new products easier as the brand name will mean customers trust new products if they have previously used a different/old product.
- Higher prices can be charged which should result in better profits for the organisation.
- Will create brand loyalty and customers will repeatedly purchase the product.
- Can mean high advertising costs to promote the brand which may negatively affect overall profits.
- However, once successful in the market place can allow organisations to save money on marketing and in turn increased profitability.
- Can be used to create an exclusive image like ASDA and George which means customers can only purchase that brand from the specific organisation.

(ii) • Generate the product/service through research and development.
- Find the appropriate finance for the new product.
- Decide if product/service meets legal requirements.
- Analyse if it is technically possible that it can be produced.
- Produce a prototype of the product/service.
- Launch the prototype on a test market in a smaller geographical location.
- Make any required alterations from the feedback given or data researched.
- Advertise the product nationwide/set a price/establish place.

3. (a) • Vertical integration is when organisations at different stages of production join together.
- Forward vertical is when an organisation takes over or merges with a customer.
- Backwards vertical is when an organisation takes over or merges with a supplier.
- Horizontal integration is when organisations at the same stage of production join together.

- Diversification is when an organisation operates in many different markets.
- Organic growth is when a firm grown from internal sources.
  - Increase in the number of outlets.
  - Increase in the number of staff it employs.
  - Opening a franchise.
- Mergers.
- Takeovers.
- Lateral.
- Conglomerate.

(b) (i)
- Increase in customers shopping at large retail parks has meant that organisations are moving from high street stores to retail parks.
- Increase in large superstores have meant many small local shops going out of business.
- Vast use of e-commerce has meant organisations now must have websites with access to online purchasing.
- Changes to opening hours means many organisations have to pay overtime to staff to work on Sundays and late evenings.
- Large supermarkets selling a wide range of products has meant customers needs can be catered for under the one roof.
- Increase in discount stores selling products at discounted prices has meant competitor organisations have had to reduce prices in order to keep customers.

(ii)
- Retailers are located closer to the customer.
- They often have an established customer base.
- They can hold stock.
- Have trained sales staff who are knowledgeable about the products.
- Will attract customers by offers of credit facilities.
- Can offer appropriate after sales services.
- Retailers buy in bulk.
- Reduced delivery cost.
- Retailers paying for advertising.
- Products displayed attractively by the retailer.

(c)
- Shares can be sold on the stock exchange meaning large amounts of finance can be raised.
- PLCs often dominate their market meaning they can force smaller organisations out of business
  - dictate market prices.
- Lenders are more likely to give money as they have greater confidence it will be paid back.
- Investors will have limited liability meaning PLCs will find it easier to attract shareholders.
- Initial set-up costs will be high resulting in poorer profit results for the first few years.
- There is a large amount of legislation which must be complied with or the company may be fined
  - have legal action taken against them.
- PLCs have no control over who buys shares which might mean investors can plan a hostile takeover.
- PLCs are required by law to publish annual accounts which will be costly to produce.

(d) (i)
- One senior member of staff (or a few core staff) makes all the important decisions.
- Decisions are therefore made quickly.
- Staff are very rarely consulted on decision making.
- Stifles staff initiative as they are not consulted.
- Is mainly used in smaller organisations.
- Employees know who they are accountable to.
- May place over-reliance on key members of staff.

(ii)
- In a decentralised structure decision making is delegated to departments whereas in a centralised structure it is made by head office.
- In a decentralised structure staff are more motivated due to empowerment whereas in a centralised structure staff can be de-motivated due to not being consulted.
- In a decentralised structure senior directors have less responsibility whereas in a centralised structure senior directors carry all the burden of decision making.
- Decentralised is often seen as being used in a flatter structure where as centralised tends to exist in hierarchical structure.
- It is harder to promote a corporate image in a decentralised structure than in a centralised structure.
- In a decentralised structure decisions can be made which only benefit one department but in a centralised structure decisions will be made to suit the whole organisation.

4. (a)
- Staff with similar expertise work together in functional grouping but in product grouping staff are organised around a specific product or service and will have different areas of expertise.
- The organisation will have functional departments which service the whole organisation whereas in product grouping each functional area will be responsible for a specific product or service only.
- In both methods departments can be more concerned with their own results than the organisation as a whole.
- Also departments may compete against each other in both forms of grouping.
- In product grouping it is easier to identify areas that are performing well whereas in functional grouping results tend to be for the organisation as a whole.
- In product grouping each department is more responsive to change but in functional grouping the organisation can become very large and unresponsive.
- In functional grouping staff will know exactly who to turn to but in product grouping this may not be the case.
- In functional grouping the organisation will have a clear structure but in product grouping the structure may be less clear and line relationships less clear.

(b)
- Finance may be restricted which might mean the organisation cannot afford to implement the best decision.
- Staff may not agree with the decision and resist the change making it less effective.
- The organisation may have policies in place that are restrictive and the decisions may need to be altered to suit policies.
- The decision may be constrained by the lack of technology and mean that new technology needs to be purchased or decisions shelved.
- Managers may not have the appropriate skills or initiative to make the best decisions and may be unable to cope with complex decisions or situations resulting in a poor decision being made
  - quality of information
  - level of risk willing to take.

(c)
- Time rate – workers are paid an amount of money per hour worked.
- Piece rate – workers are paid an amount of money per item produced.
- Overtime – once a set number of hours are worked any hours over that time is paid at a higher rate.
- Commission – workers are paid a % of the amount of overall sales.
- Bonus rate – a basic wage is paid plus a bonus for achieving an agreed level of output/profit.

- Flat rate/salary – workers are paid a set amount per month/year.
- Contract work – an agreed payment is made for a set amount of work/job.

(d) (i)
- Attainment – a candidate is given the chance to demonstrate their skills; would be used to test skills in ICT or to measure skills against a set standard.
  - Aptitude – assesses a candidates personal abilities and skills; would be used to decide if the candidate had the required skills for a job, ie, numerical skills for an accounts vacancy.
  - Intelligence/IQ – measures a candidates mental ability; used for jobs where candidates may be solving problems.
  - Psychometric/psychological – assesses a candidates personality; used to assess the candidates mental suitability for a job.
  - Medical – measures a candidates physical attributes; used for jobs such as the fire brigade that require certain levels of physical strength.

(ii)
- The vacancy can be filled relatively quickly.
  - Staff can be motivated if they see there is the chance of promotion within the organisation.
  - The managers will already know if the employee has the required skills for the job.
  - Allows the organisation to save on induction and training costs.
  - Reduced costs of advertising.
  - Can mean there is a lack of new ideas brought into the organisation.
  - The number of potential candidates is greatly reduced.
  - When a vacancy is filled it will mean another one opening up and then requiring to be filled.
  - Can cause tension amongst staff.

5. (a)
- Will improve communication through use of:
  - e-mail which will speed up sending files to colleagues throughout the world
  - can have attachments sent to colleagues to view
  - use of videoconferencing will allow meetings to take place without travelling.
- Increased access to information through the use of the Internet and access to worldwide sources will allow organisations to look at competitors' websites
  - find suppliers anywhere in the world
  - access information from anywhere in the world.
- Increases productivity and speed of work as computers often work faster than humans.
- File sharing can be carried out anywhere in the world through the organisation's network which will improve decision making as files can be shared and worked on at same time by colleagues anywhere in the world.
- Saves on costs
  - travel costs with use of videoconferencing
  - labour costs as use of computers will reduce labour requirements.
- Improves quality of product or service
  - computers will produce a consistent quality each time
  - reducing the number of errors and wastage.
- Allows for more flexible working with staff as they can work from home and stay in contact via ICT – better relationships.
- E-commerce/e-tailing

(b)
- The organisation needs to take into account the ideas/principles of the owners.
- They need to design appropriate logos, motifs and uniforms.

- They need to consider a corporate design for shops and outlets.
- They have to make staff aware of the corporate culture and image
  - this can be expensive
  - may involve staff training costs.
- Will have large cost implications for changing logos, uniforms etc throughout an organisation.
- May require the organisation to hold launch events or press conferences.
- Clearly defined policies and procedures.
- Empowerment/employee views

(c)
- Time is taken to go through the structured model and therefore no rash decisions are made.
- All necessary information is gathered which should allow for a fuller more comprehensive analysis of the information before a decision is made
  - decisions are therefore based on relevant and reliable information.
- Alternative solutions are looked at before a decision is made meaning the first solution is not accepted as the best and implemented.
- More ideas should be found as the process is followed and throws up much more ideas from employees.
- The decision must be communicated and this means all relevant stakeholders should know the decisions of the organisation and not be missed.
- The final decision is monitored and evaluated which allows for corrective action and an analysis of how effective the decision was.

(d)
- To highlight periods when cash flow will be a problem.
- This will allow corrective action to be put in place.
- Can be used to secure loans or to show investors.
- Is used to make comparisons between actual expenditure and targeted.
- Can show periods that the organisation will have cash available for major investment or purchases of fixed assets.
- Is used to give departments a budget to focus on (targets).
- Used to monitor spending throughout the organisation.
- Planning.
- Delegating responsibility to junior managers.
- Measuring performance.

(e)
- Organisations can produce products to meet exact customer requirements
  - this will mean increased customer satisfaction
  - will improve an organisation's competitiveness if they are the only one that can provide non-standard products
  - a higher price can then be charged.
- It allows the customers to change the design during the process which allows for alterations to meet customers' needs.
- The work is not repetitive and as such the employees will be more motivated with increased job satisfaction.
- The wages paid will need to be higher to reflect staff skills and this will increase the overall final price of the product.
- There can be higher than average research costs which again will be reflected in the price charged to the customer which may be off-putting.
- Costs are high as a variety of machinery/tools are required which may often be laying idle.
- Lead times can be lengthy and this means that customers cannot simply walk in and purchase the product, again this may be off-putting.

BUSINESS MANAGEMENT HIGHER 2012

SECTION 1

1. Marketing
- Expensive promotional activities were needed to keep the exclusive brand image
- High quality materials used meant high prices needed to be charged
- Increase in overseas competition
- Lower overseas pricing policies
- Spending on luxury items in UK reduced

Finance
- Could not raise the finance needed through sale of shares on stock market/Number of potential investors greatly limited
- Discussions with interested investors fell through
- No government funds available to save struggling companies
- Extravagant spending
- Went into administration

Operations
- High costs of production
- Workforce was decimated/120 redundancies
- No knitters or production staff/need to employ 60 workers in 2 months
- Old building was not suitable for modern manufacturing
- Existing machinery needed to be updated to incorporate the latest technology

External Factors
- Worldwide economic downturn
- Overseas competition
- Lower wages paid by overseas competitors
- Savage cuts in National Budget

A maximum of three points for each heading is expected.

2.
- Provide training for start-up businesses
- Business managers will give advice on financial planning
- Preparing a business plan
- Can give advice on the type of business organisation to choose
- Provide useful local contacts
- Provide free office/accommodation for a period of time
- Advice on location
- Advice on local market/competitors

3. Premium Pricing
- Choose a high price to sell the product
- This will give the customer an image of quality

Market Skimming
- Start off with a high price to sell the product
- This will appeal to a certain market segment who want the product in the introductory stage
- Allows the business to make high profits prior to competitors entering the market
- As competitors enter the market the price is reduced
- This allows people on lower income to purchase the product

A maximum of three points per tactic is available.

4. Operational
- Day-to-day decisions
- All staff including lower level managers
- Low financial risk decision

Tactical
- Medium term
- Made by middle managers
- Are taken to achieve strategic decisions

Strategic
- Long term decisions
- Shaping the objectives of an organisation
- Taken only by very senior managers
- Carry a large financial risk

5.
- In a decentralised structure decision making is delegated to departments whereas in a centralised structure decision making lies with senior managers
- A decentralised structure relieves senior managers of a lot of the daily tasks but in a centralised structure managers carry the whole burden of decision making
- In a decentralised structure subordinates are given responsibility to make decisions which is motivational whereas in a centralised structure subordinates are less motivated as decision making is made only by senior managers
- In a decentralised structure decision making is faster than in a centralised structure as local managers do not have to consult national managers prior to making a decision
- In a centralised structure procedures tend to be standardised throughout the organisation but in a decentralised structure procedures will be decided by local managers
- In a centralised structure decisions are taken for the organisation as a whole whereas in a decentralised structure decisions take into account local arrangements/customers
- In a centralised structure a high degree of corporate identity exists whereas in a decentralised structure corporate culture is harder to impose

6.
- ICT increases productivity due to the use of machinery which can allow for more products made
- unit costs reduced
- Reduces waste as technology makes fewer mistakes and this increases profit
- A consistent quality of product is made which can increase customer satisfaction
- Can mean less staff needed which reduces overall staffing costs/increases profits
- Improves the speed of communication due to the use of e-mail or intranets which makes decision making quicker
- Increases the access to information which should result in a more informed, better decision being made
- Technology can be used in situations that are hazardous to workers which results in less accidents to the workforce
- Accuracy should be increased as technology results in less mistakes especially when carrying out large calculations resulting in improved customer satisfaction

7. (a)
- To plan ahead for production/sales
- Provides targets for staff to aim for
- Actual figures can be compared to target figures
- Allows co-ordination of production quantities to match anticipated sales
- May highlight areas requiring improvement if targets not met
- Targets from budgets can be used as motivational tools for sales staff

(b)
- Use marketing measures to move unwanted stock
- Reduce the length of time given to customers to pay for goods
- Have a maximum amount owners can withdraw/reduce drawings
- Try to get increased credit terms
- Find a cheaper supplier
- Reduce wages/any other expenses
- Take out a short term overdraft
- Increase owners' own capital
- Reduce repayment of loans

8. Understocking

- Becomes harder to cope with unexpected changes in demand which means customers may go elsewhere to purchase the product if the firm doesn't have it in stock
- If customers go elsewhere they may lose them completely and not just the one time
- Production may have to stop completely as there are no raw materials to use in production which can mean paying for workers who aren't producing any goods
- Continually ordering or restocking can mean increased administration costs
    - Increased transport costs
    - Increased unit costs due to not bulk buying

Overstocking

- Carrying large amounts of stock will increase the cost of storage reducing profit
    - May result in having to pay larger insurance costs
    - Increased security costs

(Maximum of two points on stock storage costs is available.)

- Capital is tied up in stock which means that the money cannot be used elsewhere such as advertising
- The stock may deteriorate resulting in larger wastage costs
- Changes in trends and fashion will mean that stock might become obsolete and not be able to be sold
- Higher risk of pilfering

A maximum of four points in any area is available.

9.
- Can save employees on travel time if they are allowed to work from home
- Allows employees to cater for family or childcare commitments
- Employees can choose the hours that suit them to work/work at a pace which suits
- Means that the employee won't be late as they can use flexitime when needed
- Can work flexitime to cover doctor or dentist appointments
- Can save an organisation on cost of office space as less space is needed if employees work from home
- Is motivational to staff
- Can cost the organisation for staff equipment to use at home
- May mean that at certain times there are limited staff in the office
- Social relationships breakdown due to not being in the office
- Can be harder to arrange formal meetings

SECTION 2

1. (a) Advantages

- Consumers buy the product in an attempt to be the same as the celebrity
- Photographs of the celebrities are used to create visual connections to the product
- Higher prices can be charged due to the endorsement
- Brand loyalty may be created due to the endorsement
- Statements can be used in promotions to further enhance the product e.g. the official hair product of David Beckham

Disadvantages

- Can cost vast amounts of money to retain the celebrity
- If the celebrity gains bad publicity the product is also tarnished
- Product endorsement does not guarantee a quality product

A maximum of five points per area is available.

(b)
- Marketing can be tailored to specific customer's needs
- Customer loyalty can be easily built up
- There is a high level of customer care given
- The organisation can respond to the needs of customer's quickly

- Can be expensive due to high staffing costs to meet customer needs
- New staff are needed if there is a new customer grouping or product created
- Competition between customer groupings/departments can exist

(c)
- Partners increase their own investment by putting more of their own money into the business. This would mean the partners retain the same control without having to dilute control by bringing in a new partner.
- Bank loan – loan over a set period of time with interest paid back. Is a simple way of increasing finance without having to alter any partnership agreement.
- Government Grant – finance into the business from the government that does not have to be paid back
- Bring in a new partner who invests their own money into the business. This brings in fresh finance that does not stretch the original partners **or** mean the original partners have to find the funds.
- Trade Credit – increasing credit terms with suppliers. Allows for an increase in finance without bringing in a new partner.
- Debt Factoring
- Bank Overdraft
- Hire Purchase
- Leasing

(d)
- The full range of an organisation's products can be shown on a website
- Saves the firm having to have large outlets or costly high street shops to display them
- Reduces costs due to not requiring large amounts of staff
- Customers can purchase online from their own home
- Allows worldwide sales – access to global economy
- Sales can be made 24/7
- Customers can leave comments on websites
- Can make use of customer details for market research purposes by email to contact customers with promotions

(e)
- Timely – information is available when required and is up-to-date
- Accurate – information does not contain errors
- Appropriate – information is suitable to the task required
- Objective – information is free from bias
- Available – information is there when needed
- Complete – information contains all the required parts
- Concise – information is brief and to the point
- Cost effective – information is not more expensive than it needs to be
- Reliable – the source can be verified

2. (a)
- Line – the relationship that exists between a manager and their subordinates
- Lateral – this exists between staff on the same managerial level within an organisation
- Functional – this is a specialist relationship where an expert has the responsibility to manage the function for the whole organisation
- Staff – this is an advisory relationship to staff within an organisation
- Informal – exists between a level of management or staff outwith the normal working arrangements/conditions

(b) (i)
- Benchmarking – using best methods identified through best practice in industry would help raise the quality of products/services
    - Quality assurance – products are checked at certain points in the production process
        - Unacceptable products are discarded

- Quality circles – groups of workers including managers and grass root workers meet to discuss the best methods and where improvements can be made
  - Allows the actual workers doing the job to make the suggestions
- TQM – focuses on quality products every time
  - Zero defects are aimed for
  - Must have commitment of whole organisation and all workers
  - Clearly defined standards and policies are implemented to ensure quality at all times
  - Products are scrutinised at all stages of the production process
- Quality standards/marks – BSI awards are used to show quality has been approved
  - Use of trade logos – such as red Lion Mark on eggs, or woolmark, show that products have met industry standards
- Quality control – products are checked at the end of the process
- Kaizen

(ii)
- Job – is where a one off specialist product is made
  - Batch - is when groups of similar products are produced
  - Flow – is when a continuous process is used and goods move along a production line from beginning to end.

(c)
- Current ratio: current assets/current liabilities, answer of 2:1 is the accepted ratio. Allows managers to monitor liquidity levels of the business and shows the ability to pay short term debts
- Acid test ratio: current assets – stock/current liabilities, 1:1 is the accepted ratio. Allows managers to know that they can pay off debts quickly
- Gross profit ratio: gross profit/sales × 100 measures the percentage profit made from buying and selling stock. Can be used by managers to compare to the industry standard
- Net profit ratio: net profit/sales × 100 measure the percentage profit after expenses have been paid. Can be used by managers to control expenses or analyse expenses
- ROCE: net profit/opening capital × 100 measures the return on capital for investors in a business. Can be compared to other organisations or a safe investment such as using a building society to invest in
- Mark Up: gross profit/cost of goods sold × 100 measures how much is added to the cost of goods for profit. Used to ensure a satisfactory level of profit is made
- Rate of stock turnover: Cost of goods sold/average stock. Used to analyse how quickly the stock is sold. Useful for sales of perishable items

(d)
- Horizontal integration – firms producing the same products combine together. This allows for greater economies of scale which allows for lower unit costs and increased profits
  - By becoming larger they should become better known in the market and this should lead to brand loyalty and increased sales
  - They might dominate the market due to the greater size of the organisation and can then set prices and encourage customers to purchase from them through large promotional activities
  - By removing competitors they will increase sales
- Vertical integration – firms at different stages in the production process combine together. This can cut out middle men and allow the organisation to retain all profits made in the chain themselves

- Backward vertical – when a firm combines with a supplier which ensures that there are constant and consistent supplies of raw materials at appropriate prices
- Forward vertical – when a firm combines with a customer which ensures that sales are constant and can increase profits
- Conglomerate – when a firm combines with another firm in a completely different market. This means that profits can be made from a variety of markets and sales do not rely on just one industry
- Divestment
- Demerger
- Asset stripping
- Internal growth

3. (a)
- Oral – spoken word which would be used at a meeting and can be a quick method of communicating
- Written – information in the form of text, letters, memos which can be referred back to at a later date
- Numerical – information in the form of numbers or statistics which can be useful to show comparisons or exact figures
- Pictorial – information in the form of pictures can make a presentation/situation look more appealing or attractive
- Graphical – information in the form of graphs or charts can be used to make comparisons from one year to another/show trends clearly
- Quantitative – information which is measurable and can be used to give percentages/or ratings such as 5* hotels
- Qualitative – information which shows someone's opinion or thoughts and is useful when judgements or a description is needed

(b)
- Identify the vacancy
  - Carry out a job analysis – identify the tasks and duties required in the post to be filled
  - Prepare a job description – draft a description of the post being filled stating the job title, location and duties
  - Draw up a person specification – this shows the qualifications and experience required by the ideal candidate
  - Advertise the vacancy – place an advert either internally on staff newsletters or externally in jobcentres or newspapers
  - Send out application forms to candidates – application forms are completed by applicants

(c)
- Temporary – is usually for a set period of time to fill a vacancy such as a maternity leave. Allows organisations to employ workers only during the time that is required until the full time worker returns
- Full time – employed for the standard number of hours. Allows an organisation to know they will have workers in during a set period of hours each week
- Part-time – working less than the full time employees of that organisation. Is suitable for some organisations who only require workers on certain days or at certain times of the week
- Permanent – a contract of employment which runs until either the employer or the employee gives the required notice of termination. Is with the organisation continually without a specified end period
  - Allows an organisation to have a core workforce which is reliable
- Fixed term – This is a contract which stipulates a fixed and definite period that the contract will run for. Allows organisations to terminate an employee's contract whenever a job is completed or the time scale is over without any legal issues

- Annualised – a specified number of hours per year are contracted to the employee/salary is paid monthly or weekly. Allows employers to have more flexibility in matching workflow to fluctuations in demand
  - Reduces the need for overtime payments
- Seasonal – can be taken as either temporary or fixed term depending on how it is described

(d) • Specialists can be used to do the work meaning the work should be of a high standard
- Could increase costs to provide the specialisation
- However it might reduce staff costs in the area that has been outsourced as the organisation does not need to pay employees continuously
- Outsourced companies will have specialist equipment again allowing for a high degree of specialisation and a better quality product
- The service needs only to be paid for when required
- Organisations can concentrate on core activities
- Organisations can lose control over outsourced work
- Loss of confidentiality
- Cheaper/dearer to outsource the work

(e) **Advantages**
- Saves the manufacturer from making lots of smaller deliveries which saves them on transport costs
- Administration costs
- Saves the manufacturer from having high stockholding costs as a lot of the stock is held by the wholesaler
- If there are changes in trends and fashions the manufacturer will not be left with unsold stock
- Wholesalers can help label and package the product for the manufacturer which is less time consuming/less work for the manufacturer
- Retailers can buy from wholesalers in smaller amounts which can help increase overall sales of the manufacturer's product

Disadvantages
- By using wholesalers manufacturers lose control over the image of their product which could mean the product not being presented the way the manufacturer would want
- Profits are lost to the wholesaler which could be kept by the manufacturer improving their financial position

Any other appropriate advantage or disadvantage that is fully explained is acceptable.

4. (a) • Strike: employees refuse to carry out their work
- Overtime ban: employees refuse to work any overtime
- Go slow: employees work at a slower rate than normal
- Sit in: employees do not work while remaining at their workplace
- Work to rule: employees only undertake the tasks which are in their job description and do nothing else
- Picket: employees demonstrate outside the place of work

(b) • The Equality Act 2010 simplifies the current discrimination laws and puts them all together in one piece of legislation
- The act makes it more difficult for disabled people to be unfairly screened out when applying for jobs, by restricting the circumstances in which employers can ask job applicants questions about disability or health
- Any mention of the 9 protected characteristics
- Now includes workplace victimisation, harassment and bullying
- Makes pay secrecy clauses illegal
- Any mention about types of discrimination – 7 types

(c) • Maximum stock level: The level of stock that should be held to minimise costs
  - involves examining storage space available and finance required for this level
- Minimum stock level: level that stock should not fall below
  - shortages could result and production could be halted if this is not accurate
- Re-order level: the level which stock should be re-ordered at
  - takes into account usage and lead times, which is the time taken between the order being placed and the delivery of the stock
- Re-order quantity: the amount that is ordered to take the stock back up to maximum level once it is delivered
- An appropriate description of JIT system is acceptable
- Stock rotation
- Computerised stock control
- Warehousing

(d) (i) • With time rate workers are paid per hour but in piece rate they are paid for the amount of items they produce
  - Both time rate and piece rate are mainly used in manual jobs
  - Time rate is simple to calculate whereas piece rate is harder to calculate due to the amount per item calculation
  - Piece rate is an incentive to produce more items whereas time rate is an incentive to work longer hours
  - Both systems can sacrifice quality for output if workers work more hours or try to produce more products

(ii) **Commission**
  - Is a reward for the amount of a product or service sold to customers
  - Can be paid on top of a basic salary
  - Paid as a percentage of the product's sale value

Overtime
  - Normal hourly rate plus an increase for extra hours worked
  - Can be paid at a higher rate
  - Is an incentive to work more than the contracted hours

Bonus Rate
  - Employees are paid a basic rate with a bonus on top for meeting agreed targets
  - Is an incentive to produce more or work harder

Annualised Hours
  - Employees are paid assuming a basic working week of 37.5 hours
  - Employees receive the same amount each week/month
  - May have to work longer some weeks/months or less in others depending on demand

(e) • By taking the time to gather information
  - No rash decisions are made
  - Decisions are based on gathered facts and not just opinions
  - Alternative solutions are found
- By following the SWOT process ideas should be enhanced and more innovative ideas produced
- By building on the strengths and eliminating weaknesses the organisation should be in a more efficient/profitable position
- By following the process opportunities may be grasped which could have been missed
- By following the process threats are recognised and managers can be proactive in dealing with them

- It can be difficult to choose from many alternative solutions and the wrong or less effective one may be chosen
- By following the structured process ideas and initiative are stifled meaning creative opportunities may be lost
- It is time consuming to follow the process and this may cause delays in decision making
  - slower to respond to any changes in the market

5. (a) • Will involve operations in several different countries
- Has a distinct 'home' base country
- Has a global brand
- Can dominate markets across many countries
- Can have budgets that are larger than many individual countries
- Can greatly influence local economies
- Cultural variations

(b) • Profit maximisation
- Sales maximisation
- Survival – to continue to be in business, especially important in a recession
- Provision of a service
- Growth – to have more outlets, staff and higher turnover
- Socially responsible – to have a good image in the eyes of consumers or local communities

(c) (i) • Trading account – shows the gross profit over a period of time
  - Is the difference between the cost of goods sold and sales
- Profit and loss account – shows the net profit or loss over a specified period of time and takes into account all expenses
- Appropriation account – shows what has been done with the total funds available to a company. It shows the division of total funds between tax payments, investment, external loans, retention of cash balances and the distribution to shareholders
- Balance sheet – shows the value of a business at a specific date
  - Contains items such as fixed and current assets, liabilities and capital

(ii) • To check to ensure they are making a similar percentage profit. GP% or NP%
- To look at costs eg expenses
- To see if they are ripe for a takeover
- To measure the other organisations' market share
- To aid decision making

Any other valid accounting or managerial reason for using a competitor's accounts is acceptable.

(d) (i) • Introduction – the product is launched onto the market. At this stage sales will be low and costs of advertising may be high
- Growth – customers' awareness of the product increases and sales start to grow sharply
- Maturity – the product is commonplace in the market and sales are at the highest and constant
- Decline – the product has many competitors and new products will be forcing sales to decline

Development and saturation as stages are acceptable.

(ii) • Introduction – Profits will still be low, if any at all
- Growth – Profits should start to rise at this stage
- Maturity – Profits should be steady at this stage although the industry profits as a whole will be shared between many competitors
- Decline – Profits will start to fall unless efficiency is improved in distribution and production.

- May even be making a loss before the product is withdrawn altogether

Development and saturation as stages are acceptable.

(e) • Quota sampling is when an interviewer is left to find the people who fit certain categories whereas random sampling pre-selected individuals, these individuals must be interviewed
- Random sampling is an expensive technique to carry out whereas quota sampling is less expensive as the interviewer can use their judgement to find people to interview
- Random sampling limits the amount of bias that can occur whereas interviewer bias can occur in quota sampling due to being able to choose who to interview
- Product led is when an organisation produces a product first and then tries to sell it to customers whereas a market led focuses on customer wants and produces a product to satisfy them
- Very little market research is carried out with product led but in market led there is a lot of market research carried out before production starts
- In product led the organisation focuses on product testing but in market led the organisation focuses on market testing

Hey! I've done it

BrightRED
PUBLISHING

Published by Bright Red Publishing Ltd, 6 Stafford Street, Edinburgh, EH3 7AU
Tel: 0131 220 5804, Fax: 0131 220 6710, enquiries: sales@brightredpublishing.co.uk,
www.brightredpublishing.co.uk

Official SQA answers to 978-1-84948-283-7
2008-2012